LEONARD M. JOHNSON

George Washington Carver

OTHER BIOGRAPHIES BY BASIL MILLER

Martin Luther
George Muller
David Livingstone
Charles G. Finney
John Wesley
Praying Hyde
Generalissimo and Madame Chiang Kai-shek
Martin Niemoeller
Moses
Mary Slessor

George Washington Carver

God's Ebony Scientist

by

BASIL MILLER

FOURTH EDITION

ZONDERVAN PUBLISHING HOUSE
Grand Rapids, Michigan

Copyright MCMXLIII by
Zondervan Publishing House

Eight Forty-seven Ottawa Ave.
Grand Rapids, Michigan

ACKNOWLEDGEMENT

The data for this book was gathered by the author, February, 1943, from the Tuskegee Institute files, in the Department of Records and Research, where hundreds of letters, newspaper reports, magazine articles and bulletins by Dr. Carver were carefully read and used.

Moreover, I spoke to scores of people who knew this "ebony wizard" personally, many of whom had been intimately acquainted with him over a period of twenty to forty years. Out of the storehouse of their memories they also furnished unpublished stories which throw light upon the grandeur of the scientist's character. I humbly acknowledge my gratitude to this unnamed group for their assistance.

More specifically I acknowledge my gratitude to Dr. F. D. Patterson, Tuskegee Institute's president, for permission to undertake the study and encouragement during the time I was gathering my material. I am deeply indebted to Mrs. Marianna Rabb, of the Department of Records and Research, for invaluable assistance in locating the Carver files, letters and clippings, without whose help the work could not have been done.

To Dean Charles H. Thompson, of Howard University, I must express my appreciation for his aid in locating the many letters and notes which were exchanged between Dr. Booker T. Washington and Dr. Carver. Dean Thompson, doubtless the world's outstanding authority on Booker T. Washington, taught me how to become familiar with the famous Negro educator, and following him I take the license of calling the great man "Booker T." and even "Booker," as he is familiarly spoken of at Tuskegee.

My thanks for invaluable assistance goes to Dr. Robert Bell, pastor of the Tuskegee Presbyterian Church; to Dr. Claude M. Haygood, pastor of the First Baptist Church; to Tuskegee Institute's chaplain, the Reverend Harry V. Richardson; to A. J. Neely of the Tuskegee Alumni Association; to R. L. Waggoner, of the Machine Shop; to Dr. Monroe Work, founder of the Department of Records and Research; to James Lomax, private dietician to Dr. Carver; to Mrs. Sadie MacAllister, hostess of Dorthy Hall; to M. D. Sprague, librarian of the Institute; and to Dr. John W. Chenault, director of the Institute Infantile Paralysis Hospital.

Especially am I grateful to D. A. Williston, long a Carver associate, for stories found nowhere else, at whose suggestion Booker T. Washington created the department which gave the scientist his opportunity for independent research. Sitting by the doctor's grave, Williston, landscape architect, said intimately, "My one regret is that I could not furnish Dr. Carver with the 'possum meal I promised him the last summer of his life."

Likewise Dr. A. W. Curtis, assistant to the famed scientist, was of invaluable help in selecting and slanting the material, for the Memorial Life of his chief.

Mr. Edgar A. Guest and his publishers, The Reilly and Lee Company, have graciously granted me permission to use Mr. Guest's poem, "Equipment," which Tuskegee friends speak of as Dr. Carver's poem. This is from Mr. Guest's book, *Harbor Lights of Home*, copyrighted by The Reilly and Lee Company, 1928. For this I am grateful.

BASIL MILLER

Pasadena, California.

TABLE OF CONTENTS

I. THE LAD WHO WAS TRADED FOR A RACE HORSE 9

II. WASHING HIS WAY THROUGH SCHOOL........ 25

III. MEETING BOOKER T. WASHINGTON........ 41

IV. LAUNCHED AT TUSKEGEE 59

V. GROWING RECOGNITION 81

VI. THE FRUITS OF FAME........ 105

VII. EMISSARY OF GOODWILL........ 125

VIII. SETTING HIS HOUSE IN ORDER........ 145

IX. GOD'S SCIENTIST LAYS DOWN HIS BURDENS 161

Guidance Through Prayer . . .

"You see there is no need for anyone to be without direction, or to wander amid the perplexities and complexities of life. We are plainly told . . .

" 'In all thy ways acknowledge him, and he shall direct thy path.'

"Why go blundering along our poor, blind way when God had told us He will help us? . . . All we have to do is to fulfill certain conditions God lays down, and He will do His part . . .

"Life is the training school for our work hereafter . . . "

—Spoken by Dr. Carver on various occasions

L.

CHAPTER I

THE LAD WHO WAS TRADED FOR A RACE HORSE

He was born slave, this George Washington Carver. He never knew the face of his mother, nor had he one recollection concerning her, save only her tintype picture. The doors to his own past were closed. The date of his birth was no more recorded than the fact that a mare on the plantation had foaled or a sow had produced pigs. He sprang from a people who were chattel, salable produce. The women of his race where judged by their fertility, the men by their brawn. Their status was little above that of beasts.

From the outset the hurdles were stacked against him. On the ledger of his recordable assets not a single mark appeared. There was no family name to bless him with a line of famous ancestors. The only name he ever knew was that of his owners. There were to be no opportunities afforded which he did not carve with his own hands.

This was the captivity from which he launched himself into life's open doors . . .

Yet when he died the world owed him a debt of gratitude which time cannot pay. When his frail body was laid to rest in the gentle bosom of Mother Earth, deep in the South, under the shade of the Tuskegee trees he loved, the nation's leaders vied in doing him honor.

No cradle marked his beginning, yet his casket bore a floral wreath furnished by the wife of

America's wealthiest captain of industry. He was taught to lilt the freeman's song under the tutelage of Abraham Lincoln, who in signing the Emancipation Proclamation broke the shackles of slavery from him. His death so rang the muted bell of sorrow throughout our land that President Franklin Roosevelt wired the Institute to which he rightly brought fame:

"The world of science has lost one of its most eminent figures and the race from which he sprang an outstanding member in the passing of Dr. Carver. The versatility of his genius and his achievements in diverse branches of the arts and sciences were truly amazing.

"All mankind is beneficiary of his discoveries in the field of agricultural chemistry. The things which he achieved in the face of early handicaps will for all time afford an inspiration to youth everywhere.

"I count it a great privilege to have met Dr. Carver and to have talked with him at the occasion of my visit to the Institute, which was the scene of his long and distinguished labors."

The national Congress and state legislatures officially mourned his passing. Pulpits sounded with eulogies of his beneficent life, and at his death the press told the story of his rise from captivity to fame.

Between the termini of his life — his plantation birth near Diamond Grove, Missouri, and his burial at Tuskegee Institute, Alabama — were all the elements of a Shakespearean drama. It was a drama pulsating with life, pathetic with hunger, poignant with want, thrilling with achievement and crescendoing to a climax of honor and fame.

George Washington Carver was black, ebony

black, yet he so lived that men forgot his color. He was a true representative of the Negro race, and became a peer of the greatest scientists of his or any generation. So outstanding were his accomplishments in the field of agricultural chemistry that none ever surpassed him . . .

The Carver plantation, near Diamond Grove, Missouri, rang with the rifle shots of nightriders as the thundering charge of the Civil War burst upon the nation. One night early in those Civil War years, just when no one is certain, a black slave mother gave birth to a sickly baby. No record was kept of the event; not even a mark was checked in the Carver family Bible, for the plantation owner was an atheist. It was just another unnamed baby to be pawned at will that sucked the breasts of his black mother.

War days broke the cruel routine which characterized the life of the slave mother and slave babe, as nightriders, under the cloak of turbulent times, swept down upon the plantation, destroying property, stealing slaves. The marauders took with them the tiny black boy and his mother and rode off into the night. The year might have been 1865, or possibly earlier, when the event took place.

When the tumult died Moses Carver discovered that his slaves were gone, and so immediately he sent a neighbor into Arkansas to search for his property. They were as rightly his as the livestock which roamed his fields, and he wanted them back. He was not unwilling, moreover, to barter with the slave-stealers for them. When the party found the thieves, they brought word to Moses that already the mother had been traded off, and no trace of her could be found.

But the baby, too scrawny ever to grow up into a valuable slave, had until then found no buyer — for who wanted a puny slave baby who had already contracted whooping cough due to the exposure of his kidnaping? The neighbor, who had found the kidnaped child, was willing to trade the tiny bundle of slave boy for a race horse which Moses owned.

When the exchange was made the neighbor must have thought he got the better of the trade. For at the then-current valuation the horse was worth three hundred dollars, and with the Civil War raging over slave-freeing no one could tell how soon the black bit of boyhood would be declared his own master. Carver made the trade, knowing that at will the nightriders would be able to drive off the horse, as well as steal the baby, should they desire.

There might also have been a spark of human sympathy back of the horse-for-baby trade, for Mrs. Carver always indicated a strong attachment to the lad, despite his color, later going so far as to adopt him into the family and bestow upon him the family name of Carver.

The hut where the black mother gave birth to her child soon lost all significance — so the Carvers thought. Eighty years later, however, the site was destined to break into the limelight when President Roosevelt signed a bill making the plantation a National Monument, honoring thus the nameless lad and his mother. Few men, rising from a similarly humble condition, have lived so nobly as to tear the attention of Congress away from the demands of a world-engulfing war and fasten it upon the claims of their birthplace.

No other colored boy has been thus honored.

Throughout the days of Dr. Carver's life the story was popularly told that he was traded directly to the kidnapers for the race horse. However, shortly before he died he added the details of the trade to the neighbor named Bentley. Booker T. Washington, at whose insistence Carver joined the Tuskegee Institute faculty, in his *Up From Slavery* says that Moses Carver, during the Civil War days when nightriders flourished, sent his slaves into Arkansas, hoping that they might escape being kidnaped.

The husky mother, greatly loved by the Carver family, whose picture they kept for the baby we know as George Washington Carver, soon found a home, a buyer or a husband and disappeared, leaving only the sickly baby for the neighbor to bring back to the Carver plantation. When George grew older, Mother Carver told him many things about his own mother which he locked in his heart until the year of his life. She seemed to have been a sensible, hard-working girl, who loved her mistress and master and obeyed them willingly.

The Carver family long kept the bill of sale which they received when purchasing this girl whose son was to become one of the world's most famous men. She was courted by a towering black from a neighboring plantation. Later she married him and they continued to live separately on the farms of their owners. Two children were born to them, of whom George Washington was the younger. George and his older brother grew up together on the Carver plantation, freed, of course, from slavery, but bound by love to the Carvers.

When Moses Carver received the little boy, the lad was desperately ill. The sickness, through which Mrs. Carver nursed him, was the beginning of a long siege of ill health which menaced Carver for many years. During his youth he was always spindly and frail, and it was not until his late teens that he grew to even the semblance of full growth.

This weakness, however, served God's broader purpose, as previously his being bartered for a horse had done. It made it possible for the Carvers to give him more freedom from manual labors than if he had been a brawny chap, able to work in the fields and carry the heavy burdens of the plantation. It was this leisure time which sent the boy into the woods where he mastered the art of talking with the flowers, communing with nature, and through nature learned of the great Creator who was to play an exceedingly prominent part in the drama of his scientific life.

When the Carver family adopted the tiny shaver, they faced the necessity of naming him. Up until that time he had been a slave, and consequently a name was of little import, but it soon became necessary that he, now a toddler in the plantation home, receive a specific designation. One characteristic was outstanding and from this he got his name. He was always a straightforward and honest chap, ever ready to affirm in essence, "I did it with my little hatchet."

Consequently the boy-traded-for-a-horse became George Washington, named for the hatchet-bearing sire of his country.

Naming having been accomplished, it was necessary for him to earn his board and bed. Too wizened for the plow, he was shunted to the kitchen, which henceforth was to be his rightful domain. He was always a skillful kitchen lad, but never an expert outdoor farmer. He could boil and bake and stew, crochet and iron, but he never could raise chickens.

Many years later it was this lack of chicken-raising ability which almost cost him his position on the Tuskegee faculty. Booker T. Washington (as we shall later see) demanded that as head of the department of agriculture he be able to raise chickens, and when Carver could not, Booker's eyes fell upon an associate, Bridgeforth, as top hand in the agricultural work of the Institute.

Forthwith George Washington tendered his resignation.

No, he just could not raise chickens! It was not his fault. It was all Mother Carver's, for she insisted upon keeping the lad out of the fields and under her expert eye. There were plenty of people, later decades revealed, who could raise a brood of chickens to catch the eye of Tuskegee's famous founder, but there were few, if any, who could go into the laboratory, and with its brewing pots and crucibles speak to the peanut and discover its secrets.

Mother Carver did it all by starting the lad's feet toward the laboratory instead of the chicken pen. That is, she was God's instrument in so directing his path that he early learned the intricate mechanisms of bean brewing, chicken frying, soup ladling. To me all of George W.'s (as he usually signed his notes to Booker T. Washington and others) years spent in Mother Carver's kitchen brigade seemed meaningless until, recently at Tuskegee Institute, while I was gathering the data for this book, R. L. Waggoner, long an associate of Dr. Carver, and head of the Institute's machine shop, told me a story that harked back to Carver's frying days.

"George W. came into the shop," said Waggoner, one night while I was visiting the shop where he was overseeing a government-sponsored training course in welding, "several years ago" — which when I pinned him down proved to be in 1934 — "and said, as he usually did, 'R. L., here's a design which I wish you would make for me.' I looked at it and it seemed to be a rough sketch of a newfangled frying pan. 'And what's it for?' I asked. Carver said, 'I'm trying to discover a method by which you can fry the bacon of a peanut-fed hog so it will not curl.' "

The scientist, so Waggoner related, went on to explain that peanut-fed bacon has a tremendous tendency to curl, and Carver wanted to teach it how to stretch out in the pan as gentlemanly bacon ought to do. This unusual interest had its birth in the plantation kitchen.

"Many were the times," Waggoner continued, "that he came to the shop with some crude drawing, the design of which I was to guess at, he wanted me to make so he could improve some product he was then working on."

He mastered other woman-sponsored techniques during these childhood years. It was not long until "the missus" had him handy with a needle and thread, and almost before he was tall enough to reach up to the ironing board he made the working acquaintance of the old-fashioned sadiron. Both of these proved welcomed additions to his collection of practical and near-scientific implementations; for during Carver's high school and college days, both sadiron and wash tub defrayed his living expenses, and even to the end of his up-and-about life, he insisted upon doing his own laundry, at least ironing his shirts and caring for his personal wear.

One who has seen his many pieces of beautiful crotcheting, the intricate designs of which he brewed in his own mind, and which are now displayed in the Carver Museum, is amazed at his deftness in needle-work. This ability also was a result of Mrs. Carver's early training.

Many other useful things sprang from those sickly kitchen days of young George, such as freedom from restraint and the regularity imposed by life indoors. There were times when he was free to roam the woods, hunt out the flowers, seek to know the secrets which nature hid from the mere passers-by. He learned the birdcalls, and though he never deprived anything of its natural liberty, still he would follow birds to their nests where he peeped in on their home life.

The trees and grasses on the Carver plantation furnished the basis of his course in botany, and though beginning early, he was to the end of his days foremost a botanist. It was as a systematic botanist that he was always supreme. One of the unfinished tasks which he laid down and left for other hands was the writing of a text in botany with the co-operation of a long-time friend and associate, D. A. Williston. Just the summer before Carver died, he told friend Williston that he would have to complete the work they had long planned together.

Though frail, there were tasks George could perform, such as an occasional trip to the spring for a bucket of water. There was wood to be cut, fires in the home furnace to be tended, cattle and livestock at the barn that called for his attention. These were menial tasks but the youngster begrudged every moment spent at them, for they kept him away from the woods, the fields and the flowers, not to mention the kitchen — which was assuming an important role in his thinking.

Peering back into his youthful past, I tried to discover a time when the lad was not religiously inclined. Those who knew him best affirmed that "he was always religious, even from the beginning." When Glenn Clark asked him about his first answer to prayer, the then famous scientist glimpsed back through more than seventy years and recalled the knife incident.

George was always a whittler, and even in his childhood days there was a love of knives tucked away in his heart. And when he was five or possibly six, he wanted a pocketknife, for "I was mechanically minded," he says. One night while in his little bed, he thought of the Father to whom he could pray for a knife. "So I prayed the Father to send me a knife," he related, and during the night he dreamed of seeing a red-ripe watermelon which had been split in half. And sticking in one half of the melon he saw a long, black-handled knife. Even the position of the knife-bearing melon was pointed out to him in his dream, "down in the cornfield, just at the edge where the corn bordered the tobacco."

Racing to the field the next morning, he went consciously to the identical spot where the knife was supposed to be. Sure enough, sticking in a split-open melon was the knife he had seen!

Those were antic-playing days for the youngster. He loved to laugh at a trick he played upon Mrs.

Carver, which kept him from many sound threshings he deserved. When he was young, he tells us, "I learned that when I had done something I shouldn't that if I cried real loud when Mrs. Carver came to whip me, Moses Carver would say, 'What are you doing to that poor child?' And that would be the end of the threshing. Consequently I got only two lickings in my life."

With a twinkle in his eyes, he told it latterly, "That wasn't because I was angelic, but because I knew how to yell."

He was all boy, though a weakling, and he loved to slip out at night after the rest of the family had gone "to bed with the chickens." He would roam the woods, going many times to a persimmon tree near by, but always on returning he found Mrs. Carver waiting for him with a handful of willow switches.

"The little black boy lived and used his freedom," says Booker T. Washington in telling of him, "to wander about in the woods, where he soon got on good terms with all the insects and animals in the forest, and gained an intimate and . . . personal acquaintance with all the plants and flowers."

It was then that he began to show an aptitude for the selection of colors. Early he learned to sketch the flowers which his morning meanders brought to his hands, and it was here he laid the foundation for his career in art. Had his science not overcrowded his art, he would doubtless have been one of his generation's greatest painters. So beautiful and artistic were his paintings that the famous Luxemburg Gallery on the Continent sought one to grace their collections.

While yet at Ames, Iowa, before coming to Tuskegee, he was declared "one of Iowa's greatest artists." He even exhibited many of his works at the World's Columbian Exposition in 1893. While in Simpson College, as we shall see later, he studied art under Etta Budd, who helped give direction to the genius for color which was native in youthful George.

While Carver was yet a child, his drawings of flowers and other forms of plant life were so perfect that those who viewed them were amazed at his ability to put on paper what his eyes saw and his hands handled in nature.

He was not only interested in seeing and sketching plant life in these youthful years but he early became known as a plant doctor. His skill in handling sickly forms of plant life approached wizardry. While young, he found his way to the woods, where he cleared a spot in the timbers, and after making a complete collection of the neighboring plants arranged them in the form of a botanical garden. Carver's fingers possessed a magic power for healing and raising plants. He was unusually successful in whatever he decided to produce, to set out, or plant. His gardens were always protected from blight, disease and insects.

"He became so expert in making all sorts of things grow . . . that he got the name of 'the plant doctor.' "

This was his God-given talent bursting into life, and out there in the fields as a boy, we see the man in embryo. Recently while in Tuskegee, a young college graduate told of driving some of her out-of-town friends around the Institute. Out on the country lane, early in the morning, they came by an old Negro tenderly fondling the plants and examining the earliest bursts of bloom.

Said the out-of-towner, "Look, there's an old colored beggar."

"Not beggar," returned the Tuskegee miss, "that's the famous man who talks with the flowers."

This art of flower-talking came to George while he was just a lad on the Carver plantation, yet it formed the springboard from which he leaped into world renown as the man to whom all forms of plant life, even the flowers, yielded their secrets. It was the man-in-the-lad that made the boy botanist, and the lad-in-the-man that produced the famous scientist. Such a mind as his could not be crowded into the thick-skulled head of an ignorant black boy. It must burst all barriers, and when there were no opportunities create its own. That is what George did.

There were a few relics he gathered from his long-lost past, which he preserved in his Museum at Tuskegee. One is a lantern he used when as a child he fed the horses and cows in the Carver barn. Another is a broken plate from which he ate in those beginning days, and by its side the old-fashioned fork from which he took his food. Also he kept an old spinning wheel, through the courtesy of the Carvers, on which his black mother spun flax and cotton during the plantation slavery days.

That was his simple and crude beginning. Late in his life he found a poem which became a favorite while speaking to college youth across the nation, and wherever he went, in the South or the North, speaking to college youth who were white or their dark-skinned brothers, he would quote it; for it emblematizes perfectly the beginnings which marked his own life.

I stopped a Negro boy on the Institute grounds,

and asked him his remembrance of Dr. Carver. Immediately he began quoting the recently buried scientist's favorite poem. They all heard it, for to George Washington Carver what God had enabled him to achieve they also could do. The poem is by Edgar A. Guest and is entitled "Equipment."

> Figure it out for yourself, my lad,
> You've all that the greatest of men have had:
> Two arms, two hands, two legs, two eyes,
> And a brain to use if you would be wise,
> With this equipment they all began.
> So start from the top and say, "I can."

My particular copy of the poem was handed me by R. L. Waggoner, machine shop foreman at Tuskegee Institute, who said in offering the stained paper, which had been typed either by Dr. Carver or his secretary, "I've heard him quote it many times during the long years of our acquaintance. He gave me this copy thirteen years ago. This poem is in reality the man."

> Look them over, the wise and the great,
> They take their food from a common plate,
> And similar knives and forks they use,
> With similar laces they tie their shoes,
> The world considers them brave and smart,
> But you've all they had when they made their start.

So familiar are these lines on the Institute campus that they are referred to as "Dr. Carver's poem." True enough, this famous man whom the world reveres for his achievements in food chemistry started life with little more than "two arms, two hands, two legs, two eyes, and a brain to use . . . " With this equipment the world's great began, and youthful George, looking about him, shouted, *"I can!"*

Rereading the Bill of Sale for his mother Mary, which Moses kept, George Carver at the height of his fame had just reasons to shout to other youth, "*You can!*" The Bill of Sale reads:

> Received of Moses Carver seven hundred dollars in full consideration for a Negro girl named Mary, aged about thirteen years, who I warrant to be sound in body and mind and a slave for life . . .

This was dated October, A.D. 1835. Carver had come out of a slave home and climbed the stairs to fame and Christian service.

He built his career upon an earnest search for the will of the Creator and a careful study of the Bible, which he was given during his high school days in Olathe, Kansas. That Word of God became the basis of his future life; he looked to it for guidance and believed it with all his heart.

L.

DR. CARVER'S PHILOSOPHY . . .

You can triumph and come to skill,
  You can be great if you only will.
You're well equipped for what fight you choose;
  You have arms and legs and a brain to use,
And the man who has risen great deeds to do
  Began his life with no more than you.

—Quoted often by Dr. Carver to students fighting their way to the top, from Edgar A. Guest's poem.

Chapter II
WASHING HIS WAY THROUGH SCHOOL

The spring of George Washington Carver's ambition started to unwind from his earliest woodland-searching years. Nature began to speak a language which he interpreted as coming directly to him, and each word spoken, each sentence of truth revealed lured him deeper into the secrets which the Creator had hidden in the flowers, the trees and all living things of the fields. George's youthful mind had the ability to grasp truths which to others were covered by the petals of the roses and the leaves of the flowers.

There was something in him that drove him farther in this quest for knowledge. The Civil War ravaged his section of Missouri, and the Carver plantation found itself with few opportunities for either fortune or education. So schooling for the black "plant doctor" was out of the question. But when he saw books he knew they locked treasures between their pages which he wished to explore. Each one became as a pirate's chest filled with diamonds of knowledge and nuggets of information which he desired to possess.

The key which was to unlock all these mental and spiritual riches was found in an old, dog-eared blue-backed speller which the plantation afforded. George W. began in dead earnest to devour the contents of the magical book which in the end was to lift the sky-line of his own mind to include the great world of learning. He literally consumed the book, lying on his stomach in the log hut which he called home. Long hours he spent in communion with the spelling forms, and his active mind retained the spelling of the words, even if it did not absorb their meaning. Day by day, belly-down on the rude boards before the open fireplace, his frizzle-haired head bent to the task, he went through the pages one by one until at last the book's contents were mastered.

Arising from this book-eating process, he looked about him for more mental worlds to conquer, and though the woods called, his plants begged for attention, his botanical garden clamored for his time and the investment of his talents, he cocked his head and caught a new call, which seemed to come from some far-off world, to walk into its lanes and master it. It was then that George became discontented with merely being a kitchen boy, a handy lad about the house. The kitchen stove lost its allure for him. The water pail no longer beckoned with an inviting smile as though to say, "Tote me to the spring where you can commune with the flowers . . . "

The world of books and schools was just beyond the edge of the familiar plantation and George must be on his way.

So with a good-bye on his lips to benefactor and benefactress, he pointed his bare feet toward the neighboring community of Neosho, Missouri. Neosho beckoned because it was to him the Promised Land, in which a little log schoolhouse was situated. And though ill equipped, to George it was a near-heaven of learning, for at least it held books and was taught by a master who could unlock their sealed contents to his mind.

At the time he was ten, and had never before seen

into a schoolhouse, his only dip into "book larnin' " being his glorious adventures in the magic realms of the speller. Leaving the plantation, he did not cast a wistful eye over his shoulders as he trod the dusty road to his land of future delight. He said as he supposed a formal and final good-bye to the folk who until that time had been as father and mother to him. He did not know how long it would take to master this new world of learning, but he determined to stay all his life at the task if this be necessary.

Barefooted George, the dust spilling from between his toes as he tramped the miles to the schoolhouse, was motivated by a sentiment which Dr. Harry Richardson, Tuskegee's chaplain, expressed recently in a memorial chapel talk on the famous scientist. "He learned that life bends to the hand that persistently pushes against it," said the chaplain. Tuskegee's students listened intently as their spiritual adviser led them to the open door of Carver's life and bid them enter and explore the forces which made him great.

Ten-year-old George W. could not have expressed the pulling force which drove him onward so beautifully as did the Harvard-trained chaplain, but a powerful and compelling something in his soul urged him on the upward road that in the end made his name a beloved favorite in America.

The seats were rough-hewn, the benches hard, and the old pine-knots of learning that he must split with his mind tougher still, but George determined not to be outdone in this task of filling his head with the white man's learning, which until then had been closed to the colored boy whom Granddad Time had yanked off the plantation by the nape of his mental neck and deposited firmly on the book-learning benches.

Though he had arrived at the school, his problems were not by any tilt of imagination solved. Town-living he was soon to discover in the uncomfortable way demanded an important something of which he possessed not an iota. It took money to live off the plantation and until then he had forgotten about this item in his equipment. Where to stay confronted him the very first night. He could bench-down on the school's log seats by day, but custom forbade him from bedding-down on them at night.

Searching the neighborhood for a spot big and warm enough to lay his frail body that first night, he discovered an old stable, and always a friend of animals, he made himself comfortable with the other inmates — which were horses. He did not look upon this as a handicap at all. He was inured to difficulties, for it had only been a few short years since he was a slave, and his people knew the sting of trouble's lash.

The stable became the only home he knew for several days. Eating likewise proved a problem, for he soon learned that a filled head was in no wise satisfactory to an empty stomach. After school hours he spent his time going from neighbor to neighbor picking up what odd tasks he could find, which usually were sufficient to provide a meal.

His ingenuity came to the attention of the Watkins family, who invited George to make his home with them in return for what menial services he could render. He was not slow in taking advantage of this offer. Moving from the stable to the Watkinses' house proved no difficulty, for he carried his possessions on his back, and more virtually all his personal wardrobe.

George saw to it that he made the best house boy a ten-year-old lad could be, and whatever either of the Watkinses wanted, he always did with alacrity. There was not a slow or lazy bone in his body, even though all of them were cut to a number six or less size when they should have been scaled to match a ten.

It was not much of a school as measured by current standards, but to George's mind it was perfect. The backless benches were no handicap to a lad who knew how to bury his head in a book. It was not his back that he had come there to educate, but his mind, and whatever the problems, either physical or social, he faced them with a strong mental resolve to master them.

While that little log building seemed to bound the entire world of knowledge, it only took this ambitious underling a year to conquer all its realms. He did not dabble around the edges of this education-pool, but plunged into its depths and came out victorious. When at eleven he realized that he out-mastered the schoolmaster in bookishness, to say nothing of the ability to converse in the mystic language with which God had made nature articulate, George was not content to stay longer in the confines of that little log mind-polishing mill.

He looked at the road which led out of town toward Kansas, and though he did not know which way he was headed, he planted his feet once more upon the highway that was to lead him to a new kingdom which he must possess. It was a long road with many a winding, and coming upon it he saw a wagon, pulled by a team of mules, which was headed in the direction in which his inner self was urging him to go.

This was his first attempt to hitchhike himself into an education. Whether he used his thumb or no in asking for the ride, the farmer *whoaed* his mules, told George to climb in, clucked the team on, and George W. was on his way around the bend of his life's road to the next great adventure — a school at Fort Scott, Kansas.

As the mules' ears bobbed along that country road and their tails switched at the flies, George rode for several days in the wagon with the feeling of a conqueror. Arriving at the mule team's destination, the steel-brittle lad clambered down from his perch, shook the kinks from his bended legs, and clenched his mental fists as if to say, "Town, here I come, and I'm on my way!"

Having toughened his mental resolve by a year of providing for himself, he did not find the task of securing board and lodging in Fort Scott so difficult a problem as it previously had been. Mother Carver, the plantation "missus," could have given him no better training than she did when she introduced him to the intricacies of stewing kettles, frying pans and Dutch ovens, not to speak of the wash tub and its rub board, the iron and the scrub bucket.

George found himself master of a trade which knew no depressions, and he was certain that as long as there were lazy white folk, and unskilled ones as well, there would be a place in someone's kitchen for a black boy who could conjure up a meal of corn pone, done to a genuine Southern brown, Southern fried chicken, with gravy slightly less dusky than his own carbon-hued face. So he marched the streets, knocking on doors, smiling at eleven the famous smile which at seventy-nine still marked him and split the black of his face to reveal the most even set of pearly white teeth one had ever seen.

His story was simple. He was there to barter his kitchen ability, small as he was — almost peanut-sized — for a place to sleep at night and something to eat between times. "Yes, I am here," he said in a frail high-pitched voice which remained characteristic of him to his last working days, "to get an education . . . " — "Yes, ma'am, I can cook, mend, bake and darn . . . Just give me a chance, is all I ask."

The good spirit of him wormed its way into an open door, and a kind lady said, "Come in . . . " Here again his life fell into the familiar plantation routine — washing clothes, taking his turn at the kitchen stove, looking a stack of dirty dishes in the face and saying, "Careful, suh, here comes the best dish-washer in the state!" He swept and scrubbed, cleaned rugs, deloused the family dog, served as private nursemaid to sows in the art of increasing Kansas' pig population.

Where opportunity presented he held old bossie's tail between his spindly legs while persuading her to give just one "tiny drop more of rich cream." Early in his career he learned that the most important drop was this last one, and when Booker T. years later invited him to Tuskegee to head the Institute's department of agriculture, he told the famous educator that the barn boys were not "stripping the cows clean enough."

The practical farmer in him, even at eleven to fifteen, whispered that if he was to hold his job with the white family while going to school, whatever he did must be done with the highest skill and ability. He became professional in this attitude, never allowing for a moment anything to be done in any manner other than the best possible.

Fort Scott's facilities for burnishing his mind were far superior to those of the little log education factory in Missouri, and he took advantage of them as time afforded. Town folk were more insistent upon longer hours of work, more strenuous tasks, and greater burdens than the country Watkinses who had sent him through the Neosho school.

Time was the commodity of which he had the most, and so long hours made no difference. It was his will to win which he must keep dominant and at the highest level. This he did, whether washing his way through school, milking himself into the status of an educated colored boy, or beating the dirt out of the rugs belonging to white people, who decades later would have felt highly honored to be his house boy.

George found school-going not quite so simple as during his first educational lap, but he made the best of his opportunities, and the mind that had mastered the log school curriculum in a year took seven years to wade through the town high school course. But he stuck at it, plugging away under the dim light of a barn lantern or the smoky light of some friend's parlor until he was in absolute possession of the courses which the school offered.

His mind was retentive then as always, and he possessed the knack of going to the heart of problems, whether of botany or high school mathematics. At the sciences he became proficient, according to the learning standards of those times — almost seventy years ago.

It was during these days that he learned how to make others think of him not in terms of color but of ability. In talking to George Washington Carver, whether the great scientist was eighty or eighteen, one never thought of his black skin, but of the fact that he was vitally alive mentally, and could converse on whatever topic he chose. His keen mind lifted him above the color-line, and but few times was this raised as an issue in his life: once when the University of Iowa, having admitted him by mail, rejected him on discovering that he was a Negro, and again decades later when a New York City hotel refused to honor a reservation for a room which they had previously accepted.

People who knew George in those earlier days recall vividly this ability to cross the color-line and become accepted as one possessing a status equal to theirs.

Due to a tragedy in Fort Scott, George wandered through Kansas, stopping at such towns as Paola, Olathe and Minneapolis. Often without money "to buy a postage stamp," he always took time for high school studies, literally "washing" his way through.

High school days over, his diploma, received from Minneapolis, Kansas, tucked under a black arm, he prepared for his return to the plantation on which he had been as a slave. Seventeen at the time, he was still so peanut-sized that when he presented himself at the depot to buy a ticket the agent sold him a half-fare one, judging him by size to be under the legal age requiring him to pay the full fare. On boarding the train, this high school graduate was greatly chagrined when the conductor thought him too small to travel alone. It was only after some insistence that he persuaded the train master that he would reach his destination safely.

For eight years he had been away from the familiar haunts, the spring house, Mother Carver's kitchen and Moses' barn, no less his own retreat in the woods where he learned the lessons of exploration which his Creator there taught him. The family was happy to welcome him to its bosom. They, too, had missed the black boy upon whom they looked as a member of the household. They were insistent that he tell them of all the kinks and turns in the grand road of his royal adventure.

Long hours he spent around the evening fire relating his struggles, and opening to them the treasure of his new-made mind. He put it all in — the barn where he slept and the friendly horses, how much milk the Kansas cows gave; and possibly it was while talking to his former owners that he realized the distinction "between good rich Jersey milk and just plain boardinghouse milk," for when he went to his laboratory decades later and the Creator told him to make milk from the peanut, he asked, "Mr. Creator, shall I make rich Jersey milk with cream or just plain boardinghouse milk?" Of course the Creator's emphasis was on the Jersey variety.

And today, many years after this occurred, Gandhi, the famous Indian leader frequently in the headlines because of his weeks-long fasts and his national leadership of India, keeps with him constantly Dr. George Washington Carver's formula for making milk from peanuts, and uses it as a regular item in his vegetarian diet; for the cow-milking George, when he walked through the open door of later experimentation, discovered how to make milk from the peanut — rich milk in which there was thick cream that could be churned into nutritious butter which ranked high in fat tests.

It was on this visit that George begged of Mrs. Carver the old lantern he used as a little boy about the barn, and the spinning wheel on which his mother wove the cloth for the plantation clothes. He asked also "for a plate from which I ate while a slave child." They were all cracked and broken, but "the missus," sensing that here was a more-than-usual colored boy, gave him one, along with a fork that he had used back in the time when they owned him body and soul.

That was a happy summer George spent with the Carvers on the familiar grounds of the plantation. He renewed his acquaintance with the flowers, took time to walk leisurely in the fields and commune with the Creator. He recharged the batteries of his ambition while talking under the soft glow of the evening stars with the family who thought more of him than of an old race horse that had seen better days.

Talking done, George in the early autumn began the trek back to Kansas, sensing that he was but at the halfway mark of his educational career. When he finished high school, he had learned of colleges from his friendly teachers — colleges where a student could study to his heart's content and master all that man knew concerning flowers, plants and all forms of botanical life. He knew, when this vision dawned, that he must be about his Creator's business, which to him was reading the mind of the plants and so living with them that later he would have a piercing insight into their very lives.

This is what he did, for the time came when he was able to diagnose the disease of plants as accurately as a physician diagnoses the disease of a human patient. This was the vision which held him captive to the end, and thrilled by the thought of achieving it, he knew the plantation, glorious as would have been a life spent amid its familiar surroundings, held no charm for him.

Back in Minneapolis, he wondered how he could best utilize the friendships he had formed in the city, and it struck him that the white folk needed a town laundry where their soiled linens would be washed clean. His first task was to secure a building and soon he announced the opening of the "George Washington Carver Laundry Service." This he did seriously. He determined that he was going to secure an education at any price, and if he could wash his way through school, this was as honorable as sweeping out the town's best bank or acting as a horse manicurist at the local livery stable.

There remains for us no record of his laundry difficulties such as mixing up the town's richest family's wash with that of someone who might live a little too near "the other side of the tracks"; but rest assured there must have been times when his rubbing took the buttons off the banker's shirts or he failed to get just the right proportion of starch or bluing in the blouses of the town's most aristocratic lady, and I expect colored George was called a few names by such folk.

Nevertheless he doubtless did the finest laundry work in the city, for he mastered the art of collar starching, shirt ironing, tie making and mending so thoroughly that even to the last month of his life, when the sands of his hourglass had run to the eighty mark, he insisted on doing his own mending, and collar and shirt ironing, as well as washing, and necktie pressing (if and when his scientific mind determined that a new press to his necktie would stimulate the processes of laboratory intellection).

This was always the working of his mind. He considered the physical to be calibrated on a lower scale of values than the intellectual. When he was invited to address a Congressional committee on the peanut tariff in 1921, said one of his associates, "George, don't you think you need a new necktie to go up there?"

"Do you think a new necktie," he said in characteristic Carver strain, a twinkle wrinkling the edges of his eyes and spreading over his ebony skin, "would help me answer their questions any better?"

Suffice it to say, George went without the new necktie, and the ten-minute speech — the time allocated by the committee — grew into an hour-and-forty-minute address.

He might be the town's laundryman but his mind was in nowise bounded by the confines of a wash tub. He kept it in the clouds, dreaming of better days far ahead, planning to finish his education at some college and then launch his career in the chosen field of plant doctoring.

At nineteen he found himself still sized in the pocket-edition class of men, having never felt the upsurge of physical development. But during the next two years, Mother Nature began to feed into his system those hormones and vitamins which caused his glandular structure to so increase its output of strengthening chemicals that, to use his own expression, "I grew like a weed." By twenty-one he reached his full height — near six feet.

During George's laundry days a friend sang the

praises of a small Kansas college so loudly to him that he determined to enter the school as soon as possible. In a very neat hand, as clear and legible as anyone has ever seen, he made out an application for matriculation, listing the courses he had taken, the exceptionally high grades he had made, and trusted the letter to Uncle Sam's mailmen.

His heart struck a high note of rejoicing when the answer arrived from the college, saying, "Accepted . . . " Six-foot George, bending over the tub in his laundry, put a new vim into his elbow grease and as he took the wrinkles out of the clothes with his sadiron, he dreamed of entering school shortly.

When George presented himself at the college, the president made a disparaging remark about his color, saying that they did not receive Negro students. That college president thus closed the doors of his institution to one of the world's most famous sons.

George then took a mental tailspin into the Slough of Despond. His dream was gone, his vision had vanished, and for the first time in his life the color-line stood before him as an impossible hurdle on his march to the top. He had not yet met the "Dr. Carver poem," written by Edgar A. Guest, which said:

> You are the handicap you must face,
>   You are the one who must choose your place.
> You must say where you want to go,
>   How much you will study the truth to know;
> God has equipped you for life, but He
>   Lets you decide what you want to be.

Early in life George laid the foundation for his religious faith, which marked him to the end of his career. Mariah Watkins, one of those colored "shouting Methodists," who gave George a home during his Neosho school year, took him to the African Methodist Church she attended. The preacher, unable to read, "lived his religion," and made a deep impression upon the lad's youthful mind.

The second religious influence which turned his attention to Christ's claims upon his soul came while he was staying in Olathe, Kansas, with a devout Presbyterian family named Seymour, who twice each Sunday took the high school student to church with them. It was during this time that George gave himself without reserve to the Master, accepting Him as his personal Redeemer. He united with Mr. Seymour's church, and remained affiliated with the denomination throughout life.

During this time he was given the little Bible which he carried throughout his long and glorious career, and to the end this remained on his Tuskegee desk. The Bible, which he believed to be the Word of God, became the foundation for his marvelous success.

L.

One of the World's Richest Men . . .

"Fifty years ago he entered this town with all of his earthly possessions tied up in a small pack.

"Today he is one of the richest men in the world. Not in natural wealth. He has chosen to give away what has come to him and has escaped the handicap of material riches . . .

"Among the cherished memories that Simpson College will always possess is the consciousness that it did not fail him when he came knocking for admission. It will always rejoice . . . that it did not make race or color the basis for entrance."

—Spoken by Dr. John Owen Gross, President of Simpson College, in 1941, when Dr. Carver delivered the Commencement Address

Chapter III

MEETING BOOKER T. WASHINGTON

Absolutely certain of entrance at the university, George spent all his money for carfare to the institution, and on arriving those tragical words, "We don't take niggers here," rang in his ears. Ordinarily he was never one to be discouraged by a temporary upset, but this almost proved more than he could take. It seemed that all the earth had slipped out from under his mental underpinning. He had no money with which to go back to his laundry in the friendly Kansas town, and so he began where he always did when seeking a new opportunity.

He set about looking for odd jobs by which he might live. One of the first jobs was to clean a rug; and it is doubtful if anyone ever did a more thorough job of it than he. This was followed by his becoming a cook for another family. Never long content to work for others since he had first tasted the joy of being his own boss, he decided to open a laundry where the students could have their washing and ironing done.

Later George abandoned his laundry project, working temporarily for a true friend, Mrs. John Beeler, whose husband owned a fruit farm south of Highland. The government had opened for settlement the Western plains of Kansas, to which young Frank Beeler had migrated, and in 1886, George followed him to Ness County where he filed on a homestead. Two years later on June 25, 1888, he proved upon his claim, mortgaging it for three hundred dollars. With this money he set out for Iowa to make a new start.

With little money but a storehouse of newly acquired experience, Geo. W. (as he often signed his name during these earlier years) went to Winterset, Iowa, where as cook at the hotel he made many new friends. As was his custom, on Sundays he attended a local church, and when the familiar songs broke from the organ, George lifted his voice and sang with the congregation.

That beautiful, mellow voice reached the ears of the church soloist, Mrs. Millholland, and she could scarcely contain herself until she had forced her husband to go to the hotel and invite the colored cook to visit them at their home. The following evening George found himself in the home; and standing beside the piano as his hostess played, he sang for her. Recognizing the unusual quality of his voice, Mrs. Millholland offered to give him singing lessons.

Never willing that an opportunity for self-betterment should pass, the cook-turned-singer accepted this gratuity, and as long as he remained in Winterset, he went regularly to the home for his lessons. The family also learned of his rapidly unfolding artistic ability and encouraged him to continue his painting. He could not forget, however, his intense desire to attend college, and during his summer's work, he met a young student from Simpson College, located at Indianola, Iowa, who was taking special courses at the State University.

As the young student listened to George's story,

he realized the unjustness of what the university had done in making color a line of discrimination for entrance, and insisted that George try to open Simpson's doors. "I have always felt," Dr. Carver said decades later, "that this was the Lord's leading. I do not believe that 'things just happen.' Through the young man I was led to Simpson where all my life's work really began."

Fifty years later when the president of Simpson visited Tuskegee Institute, Dr. Carver showed him through his museum, and after explaining the various items to the educator, he said, "All of this resulted from the vision I received at Simpson College." "In just what way," asked the president, "do you mean this?"

"It was at Simpson," answered the scientist, "I realized that I was a human being . . . "

This was the dawning of his recognition that he had all the physical blessings possessed by the great men when they began their upward climb toward fame — two hands, two eyes, two legs and "a brain to use." Arriving at Simpson late in the eighties, he went to work with a will to win. He was destined to spend the happiest three years of his life up to that time in the college where he took the usual academic courses, his heavy emphasis being upon botany and kindred subjects.

After matriculating and paying his fees, he discovered that only ten cents remained in his pockets. Counting the coins over and over in nowise stretched them, for they always numbered the fateful ten. But George was no stranger to hardships and with this ten-cent lead over his other educational ventures, he felt himself rich indeed. Nor was he long in perplexity as to how best to invest the money.

He had not acquired expensive appetites, nor reached the "rich Jersey cream" stage in his life. Going to the store, he bought a nickle's worth of suet and then turned to the other counter and invested his remaining fortune in corn meal. To George, suet and corn meal were food fit for a king. Returning to his room, he began concocting a suet-meal diet sufficiently nourishing to keep his body active and his mind keen.

Referring to that first-Simpson-week diet, he says, "I wouldn't exactly call it the finest on earth, but it was enough when there is a will to get ahead."

The problem of lodging was soon solved when a kind old lady offered him the use of her woodshed in which to live. "After all," the youthful giant reasoned, "a woodshed makes a better home than a stable." Having started out his educational career in a horse barn, he felt elated that he could get so high as the woodshed. Living was simplified when he discovered that there were boys at Simpson with more money than grit, and others without the knack of knowing how to wash their clothes. So he bought on credit a wash tub and a board, and with the loan of an old iron he set up his own college laundry.

He was not above acting as advance agent and promotional manager for the "Carver College Laundry," and he went forth to drum up business. Having trained himself to do thoroughly whatever he undertook, he was soon able to get a few washings done for college lads and let them act as his living advertising boards, and it was not long until there was enough work to consume all his spare time. By this means he kept his bills paid at the college, and soon accumulated enough surplus cash to lift his daily menus to a higher level than the customary suet-meal diet. An occasional pork chop began to appear in that section of the woodshed which functioned as kitchen-dining room.

George W.'s genial smile wormed its way into the boys' hearts and soon the old woodshed-laundry rang with the merry voices of the college lads as they visited with their collegiate male washerwoman. Cold weather created a problem, but by the time of the first ice the laundryman had enough money or credit to purchase a stove, and here he worked throughout the winter. When not busy attending classes at the college or studying in the library, he was whacking away at the rub board.

While here in college, George entered the art class and studied painting under the direction of Etta Budd, who headed the art department. His proficiency with the brush, his deftness in color discrimination soon won friends and attracted attention, and many of his most beautiful works were either begun or finished during this time.

At Simpson he also studied music or at least gave attention to his singing and learned to play the organ. Throughout his life these avocational interests held a high place in his thinking and were constantly demanding his attention. During these earlier years, even after he had been at Tuskegee for some time, he always aimed to make his career that of art, with music as a sideline. After Carver joined the Institute staff he wrote a note to Booker T. stating that he wanted shortly to resign from his agriculture teaching and devote himself to art that he might show the world a Negro could climb as high and shine with as much luster as his white brothers in this field.

After his junior year at Simpson he decided to enter the Iowa State College at Ames, where he could give his attention more completely to botany and allied sciences. He could never free himself from this intense love for plant life. It revealed itself in his art, for virtually all his paintings are of flowers, plants and beautiful landscapes where trees abound.

On arriving at Ames, he faced the old difficulty of finding a place to stay, and though he had money to pay for it, he was refused a room on account of his color. But this was no impossible hurdle for him to take in his stride, for he had determined to devote himself to agricultural chemistry that he might benefit his own race. He had begun to hear, while at Simpson, the divine call to his people.

As always, the slight embarrassment of not being welcomed into a rooming house or a home proved a blessing in disguise. On the faculty was James Wilson, director of the Agricultural Experiment Station, who on hearing about the Negro student's condition, said to him, "George, you may stay in my office." Immediately the office was fixed for Carver's sleeping quarters and George moved in.

This proved a valuable and lasting relationship, for through Carver's Ames years Wilson always befriended him, and when he had received his degree, made a place on the faculty for him. When the young Negro scientist left Ames for Tuskegee and his own department of agriculture, Wilson's blessings went with him, and as the years passed the white Wilson and the Negro Carver remained true friends.

Each was destined to gain fame in his own way,

Wilson to become Secretary of the United States Department of Agriculture and Carver to arise to the position of the world's most famed agricultural chemist. When they would meet as they did at Tuskegee, the reminiscences of those Ames years were happy ones.

George at last had found the place of his heart's content and he went to his classes with a resolve to make the most of his opportunities. He devoted himself to the study of bacterial experimentation in systematic botany. It was during these Ames years in the early nineties that he laid the foundation for his future knowledge of botanical chemistry which opened to his wizardry the wonders of the peanut, sweet potato, pecan and southern clays.

While at Ames he was given charge of the greenhouses where he had an opportunity to make a firsthand scientific study of flowers and plants, following upon his childhood experiments on the Carver plantation. This firsthand knowledge of flowers also found expression in his paintings, and he placed on canvas the beautiful forms he found in his greenhouse.

His painting progressed with his other studies until some thought of him as "Iowa's ebony Leonardo"; his sketches were exhibited at the 1893 Columbian Exposition, where they attracted much attention to himself. Professor James Wilson said of them, "Professor Carver is probably the very finest painter in the state of Iowa."

During this time George joined the college battalion of the National Guards, and attained the rank of lieutenant. There was this about him: he never destroyed anything he possessed, and today one can see his lieutenant's uniform in the Carver Museum at

Tuskegee. He kept it through the years as a relic of his happy collegiate remembrances and possibly there might have been a slight touch of pride which motivated him in preserving the uniform, for doubtless he cut a dashing figure at the first World's Fair in Chicago, when he marched with the college battalion, which accompanied Governor Boies on the trip.

He always had this knack for saving; even many of his clothes in later years seemed to be vintaged in the nineties. I had heard it rumored that he wore toward the end of his life an overcoat which he had purchased during President Cleveland's administration. Wanting to check on the rumor while gathering data for this book, at the Institute I asked Captain A. J. Neely, of the Tuskegee Alumni Association, if it was true.

"I don't know whether it was the same coat or not," the captain replied, a broad grin splitting his face, "but it certainly looked like it," he added, smiling.

The Negro student proved a valuable asset to the agricultural department of the Iowa school, for his knowledge of plants was amazing. He seemed to possess the ability to touch a sick flower or shrub and immediately know what would be required to heal or restore it. This art lingered with him throughout life, and many are the Tuskegee stories of how Dr. Carver, the famed scientist, visited the yard of virtually every white family in the town of Tuskegee, (it must be recalled that the town of Tuskegee, Alabama, and Tuskegee Institute are distinct places, separated by about a mile's distance).

Going into the little city of Tuskegee, the white women would call to him, asking that he diagnose the trouble with some sick plant. The doctor would take the shrub in his hands, study it for a moment, go back to his laboratory where he concocted the proper medicine, stimulant, or fertilizer for that particular flower or shrub, and carry it back to the owner.

As he lay in state at the Institute Chapel, a beautiful camellia was in his buttonhole, as was his custom while living. This flower came as the gift of a white woman; she had picked the bloom from a shrub which he had healed many years earlier, a story which I shall reserve for the details of his funeral.

This healing art developed rapidly at Ames in the college greenhouse, under Professor Wilson's guidance and tutelage. It was not long until the professor was out-professored by his pupil, and when George W. took his B.S. degree in Agriculture in 1894, through friend Wilson's influence and his own ability, plus training, he was added to the teaching staff. He studied plants and their ills just as carefully and individually as a doctor studies each particular patient. It was this ability and diligence which opened the teaching position to him.

Nor did he lose this healing touch through the years. Wherever he went, even after fame crept upon him, he would be asked to prescribe treatment for some sick plant, as a famed doctor would be summoned to treat a sick and important patient.

The story comes to mind how in the early forties he went to New York City, and on seeing the shrubs which had been planted in the parkway on Park Avenue, at a cost of some eighty thousand dollars per mile, he took time to stop a moment, examine the shrubs, and, like a doctor who sees in a patient the ravaging effects of a deadly malady, he recognized the marks of death. He said, "They will all be dead in two years' time." He knew the malady and was willing to prescribe the remedy necessary to save their lives and prevent a mass epidemic of plant death.

It was this plant-healing technique or skill which brought him invitations to speak before or read papers at horticultural conventions throughout the state of Iowa during the latter part of his Ames professorship. In addition to his own work, he became actively engaged in the field he loved, and never did a mother nurse a sickly babe or tend a healthy one as Carver cherished the plant wards under his care.

He mastered the science of plant chemistry during this time and also became an expert in the field of systematic botany. This combination gave him the ability in the coming years to take the peanut and the sweet potato apart, find of what they consisted and then put these elements together again in the hundreds of forms he discovered from these two foods, alone. Knowing plant chemistry, he found it no unusual problem, for instance, to build the chemical formula for sweet-potato starch, as he did in his laboratory.

It has been averred that the youthful scientist was as careless of his personal attire during his first teaching years as he became later in life. But this is not entirely true, for the pictures which show him either painting or working during those early years give us a glimpse of a well-dressed man, who often wore the familiar winged collar. He cared little for money at this time or any time during his life. All he asked for was a living sustenance, for he dressed simply and he had no expensive tastes.

He soon attracted the attention of other professors in the school, among whom was one called "Old Uncle

Henry Wallace," and when Carver was given charge of the bacteriological laboratory, the greenhouse and the department of systematic botany, the grandson of Professor Wallace was a heel-dog to the colored teacher. His name also was Henry, and as a lad he would tag along after the Negro scientist, going with him as he cared for his flowers, and out into the woods, where together they searched for the hidden secrets of plant life.

Here sprang up a lasting friendship, and the little Henry, as lads are accustomed to do, grew into a stalwart man, took his grandfather's place in the agricultural leadership of Iowa, later was called to serve as Secretary of the United States Department of Agriculture, and now is Vice-President of the United States. During the years there existed a close relationship between Henry Wallace and George Carver which continued until the end. Neither recognized any color distinction for they both spoke the language of science and nature.

Around the college laboratory Professor George's fame began to spread until he attracted attention wherever he went. He made friends rapidly, and his unique personality drew people to him. Through the long years that were to come, this ability remained with him. When he addressed conferences of farmers, and spoke to botanists, he was laying the foundation for the time when he would be called upon to travel extensively and speak to large and famous gatherings of scientists, farmers, college and university students and popular groups throughout the South and elsewhere.

Search though I did, I found no single reference,

either from the Carver literature or from acquaintances whose knowledge of him ran back more than forty years, to his ever having had a lady-friend. Even at Ames, when the sap of his life ran strong, he was "devoted thoroughly to his calling, and had but one love, plant life."

While he was always courteous to the ladies, and there were many who would have courted him, he found little time for them outside of a casual acquaintance. Serious in his youthful art, he was congenial and friendly on the Ames campus as also at Tuskegee.

When he received his degree of Master of Science in Agriculture, 1896, he reached a bend in his life's road. He recognized that his formal education was finished, and that the State College had done all possible for his intellectual advancement. It was now time for him to seek a permanent place for the investment of his talents in the service of God and humanity.

During this time he was devotedly religious. In the little square-backed Bible which always lay on his laboratory table I found a small card advertising the college Y.M.C.A. at Ames, bearing the date of 1896. On it was the Scripture, "Seek ye first the kingdom of God, and his righteousness; and all these things shall be added unto you" (Matt. 6:33). On the back flyleaf of the Bible was his name; the town, Olathe, Kansas; and the date, September 25, which he had been given while in Olathe before his college days.

The still small voice of his Creator began to speak definitely to him at this time, indicating that it was the divine will for Geo. W. to devote his life to some form of service to his race. Naturally the Southland furnished the best opportunity to reach the most Negroes in the smallest area. Hence he began seeking a place in the South where he could teach.

Booker T. Washington, having founded Tuskegee Institute in 1881, naturally had attracted the attention of Negro leaders everywhere, and Professor Carver was no exception. As the young scientist began to cast about for a Southern school in which to invest his abilities in humanitarian service, Tuskegee came to mind. Early in 1896 Booker T. was to deliver an address at Cedar Rapids, Iowa, and after some correspondence he asked Carver to meet him there.

The scientist, on meeting the educator, was impressed with his seriousness and when he learned what Booker T. aimed to do at the Institute his heart warmed toward the offer of a position on the faculty. Meanwhile Washington returned to Tuskegee, where he discussed the matter of a head for the department of agriculture.

"Of course it has always been the one great ideal of my life," Carver wrote to Washington on April 12, 1896, "to be of the greatest good to the greatest number of my people possible, and to this end I have been preparing my life for these many years, feeling as I do that this line of education is the key to unlock the golden doors of freedom to our people."

Asking for a catalog of the Institute, Carver went on to say that he had already tentatively accepted a teaching position almost under the shadow of Tuskegee, "So if you are prepared to make me an offer now it shall receive my first consideration . . . May the Lord bless you and prosper your work."

On April 17, Booker replied, saying, " . . . in conversation with a member of the board a few days ago . . . it was his idea that we should be compelled to get a white man to take charge of this department, as he thought there was no colored man in the country fitted for such work . . . Now we very much prefer to have a colored man in charge of this new department, and I think you are the man for the work."

Becoming more specific, he outlined a proposition to the Ames professor, saying, "If you are willing to come here we can pay you one thousand a year and board, board to include all expenses except traveling. This perhaps may not seem a large salary but from the first we have made a policy of trying to get teachers who come not only for the money but also for their deep interest in the race."

Fearful that the Ames college had made Carver a more tempting offer, Booker added a hook to his proposition by saying that if the named terms were not "satisfactory we shall be willing to do anything in reason that will enable you to decide in favor of coming to Tuskegee."

Four days later Carver took up his pen and answered in his own handwriting, with a neat flourish to his letter, not in the least turning down the offer, but assuring Booker T. that he must decide soon whether "I am to stay here, go somewhere else in the South, or come to you." He was pleased with the spirit of the Tuskegee president's letter and said, "I am very much pleased with the spirit of your letter, and assure you if I come the money will not be the sole object, only secondary."

This was characteristic of Dr. Carver. All he ever asked was enough money on which to live, and in a survey of hundreds of personal letters between Carver and Washington on all conceivable subjects and under all circumstances not once is there found evidence of the mercenary spirit. The thousand dollars were sufficient for his needs, and in a letter to Washington fifteen or more years later he indicated that his salary had never been raised during the time.

Interesting stories circulate around the Institute concerning Dr. Carver and his salary checks. Many times it became necessary for the treasurer to hunt up the busy scientist and force him to cash his checks, so that the books might be cleared. No, money was not his sole object in going to Tuskegee.

But he did want Booker T. to know that Ames had promised him a raise in wages if he would stay with them, and he said, "I have already a position here, and one of the professors told me the other day they would raise my wages here if I would stay. But I expect . . . to go to my people and have been looking with favor for some time to Tuskegee."

He enclosed the four-year course in agriculture from which he had graduated, assuring Booker T. that his training was sufficiently broad to handle whatever problems might arise in the new position. His letterhead from the school listed him as an assistant in the department of botany. He did, however, drive home the necessity of a speedy decision on Tuskegee's part, saying, "When will it be necessary for me to come? . . . I will accept the offer. I shall await an answer with a considerable degree of anxiety as I must decide soon. May God bless you and your work."

As I read these letters in George Washington Carver's own handwriting, bearing his own signature, the very spirit of the man breathed from the time-stained pages. He walked through those correspondence files which the Department of Records and Research at Tuskegee Institute has kept through the years. Here he was forty-seven years ago, a young scientist in whom the spirit of brotherly service was strong, breathing a prayer, as he signed his letters, for God's benediction to rest upon this educational venture which was to light the way to a new era for his Negro brethren.

By April 27, Booker T. had made up his mind to have Carver at all costs and offered him the position, and on May 8, Carver wrote the president under whom he was to serve many long and fruitful years, saying, "It affords me great pleasure to be identified as one of the faculty of Tuskegee." He mentioned his collections of botanical specimens he had gathered and would be costly to move, but which would be of great service to the school. He enclosed this letter, "May the Lord pour out his choicest blessings upon you and your work. Yours for Christ, Geo. W. Carver."

A week later in writing to the Institute president, he affirmed his willingness to co-operate "with you in doing all I can *through Christ who strengtheneth me* to better the condition of our people."

The decision was made, and there is no indication on Carver's part that he ever regretted it. When the news spread throughout the State College at Ames that George Carver was leaving for Tuskegee, consternation struck students and faculty alike, for the popular Negro teacher and experimenter had won his way into their hearts.

But Carver, always religiously inclined and attuned to the Heavenly Voice, had heard God's call of service to his own race, and he was ready to go. He was now thoroughly prepared for his life's work, no longer a novice at the art of experimentation in plant chemistry. Booker T. Washington's school, although small, grew around the dynamic personality of this famous Negro, who was able through the years to interest white capitalists in his work, which resulted in their erecting his buildings and endowing his departments. Tuskegee was destined to become the Negro's outstanding training center, or at least was more insistently to claim the attention of the nation than any other institution of its kind.

Here it was to furnish Carver his opportunity to achieve for himself a justly deserved fame, yet one which he sought not. In his early days, however, "he took fame and growing popularity in his stride and flourished under it," as his friend and botanical compatriot, D. A. Williston, expresses it.

GOD'S LITTLE WORKSHOP . . .

"Here is what I call 'God's little workshop.' No books are ever brought in here. What need is there of books? Here I talk to the little peanut and it reveals its secrets to me.

"I lean upon the twenty-ninth verse of the first chapter of Genesis . . .

" 'And God said, Behold, I have given you every herb bearing seed, which is upon the face of all the earth, and every tree in the which is the fruit of a tree yielding seed; to you it shall be for meat.' "

—Spoken by Dr. Carver in one of his addresses

Chapter IV

LAUNCHED AT TUSKEGEE

Dr. Carver lost little time once his mind was made up that it was God's will for him to take the Tuskegee position. This was his first consideration. Early he had learned that success in unraveling the mysteries locked in the heart of plants came through a special sense of being rightly placed in the divine scheme of things. With God brilliant achievements were possible; without His aid, George felt he would be only another scientist blundering along the path of accomplishments.

His heart throbbed to the Tuskegee challenge, for he was convinced that here he could best serve his race. By early September he had gotten his collections together and wrote Booker T. Washington, "I will leave here about October 7, sooner if I can arrange to do so."

On arriving at the Institute, he was somewhat perplexed at the slowness of preparation being made for his housing, and wrote to the finance committee, "Some of you saw the other day something of the valuable nature of one of my collections. I have others of equal value along agricultural lines . . . " After complaining of the lack of room for unpacking and space to house his workshop, he continues, "You doubtless know that I came here solely for the benefit of my people, no other motive in view. Moreover I do not expect to teach many years, but will quit as soon as I can trust my work to others and engage in my brush work . . . "

Hence his early desire and interest was painting and not agriculture. His motive for the change from his first love, plant doctoring, to art was that he might "show to what we may attain, along science, literature and art."

There were vexations other than a lack of unpacking space for he wrote to Booker, affirming, "My room is full of mice, and they are in my boxes, doing me much damage . . . I am handicapped in my work. I wanted a medical journal the other day in order that I might prescribe for a sick animal, but I couldn't get at it."

This is little like the mature Carver, whom we meet rambling along the dusty roads of southern Alabama, picking up here a sample of clay, there a flower to be examined, which on returning to the laboratory — one he had entirely fabricated by his own ingenuity —he transformed by his wizardry, the clay into paints for one of Booker's new buildings, and from the flower extracted a perfume with which to make aromatic "a bedbug killer I have just finished preparing," as he informed the president.

At first he was impatient at delays, the lack of attention to his personal needs — such as housing room, space for equipment — and the lack of facilities, but under the shaping hand of the master builder, Dr. Washington, he trained himself to create what he lacked. He learned, as he shortly wrote, "The equipment has to be in the head of the man and not in the laboratory."

When he had mastered this idea, he was ready to be on his way to success. Booker had begun in a chicken house his work of shaping Tuskegee into the four-million-dollar plant it now is, and he knew the men who worked with him, whatever their training, must develop their facilities and build with what was at hand. He outlined Carver's program, laid out his duties, and committed to him the problems of crop raising, cattle care, production of eggs and especially of chickens. Washington's idea was to make the Negro institution self-sufficient and to train the students to take their place in the world of today.

Carver worked first to build his own laboratory equipment. This can be seen now in the Carver Museum, and consists of a few beakers made from bottles with their necks broken off, and other crude imitations of the excellent workshop he left at Ames. For a Bunsen burner, he took an old ink bottle, with a wick made of twisted string and held in place by a cork. One who visits the Museum will see a large jug, an old skillet, a medicine bottle with a glass tube inserted into it for a distillery, a teacup in which he crushed the elements used in the experiments, fruit jar lids used to hold chemicals, and similar crude laboratory substitutions.

While there was no money to purchase supplies, he felt the laboratory equipment made little difference as long as his head was filled with techniques and methods and his mind was directed in research by the Creator.

Dr. Washington, in outlining Carver's work, pointed to the grassless grounds surrounding the buildings and told him, "Our people have always seen signs, saying, 'Keep off the grass.' Do you think you can grow grass out there for them?"

Carver not only thought he could, but he did grow

grass on the Institute grounds, and transformed them into a green carpet of beauty. He had come there to make the most of the South's agricultural opportunities in order that the Negro might directly benefit by his experimentations. With this end in view he went to work. There was much to be done. The farm land was poor and needed the stimulation of a new soil. He took baskets and went to the woods where he found rich loams which he toted back to his experiment plots. He knew he must make a scientific analysis of Alabama's soil before he could rightly attempt to produce more and better crops from it.

To this end he tramped the fields, visited neighboring farms, gathered handfuls of earth, scraped dirt into pans and, returning to the laboratory, gave it a scientific scrutiny. When he was through he knew just the elements which must be added to the earth before it would be in the best possible condition for crop production.

The practical-minded president did not let a single thing escape his attention and he constantly dogged Carver's steps with notes from the office with suggestions, bordering on commands, as to what he should do. On October 4, 1897, for instance, he commanded the professor to "look over the Marshal farm and report to me as soon as possible any recommendations you see fit to make." Three weeks later he asked Carver "for a list of all possible shrubs that can be planted to advantage on the grounds." Then came a fence to be fixed "per order." By the middle of November of that year, the president was dissatisfied with the milk reports which were coming to his office and turned them over to Carver for proper action.

During the next year Geo. W., as he signed his

notes to the president, took time to complain that he needed someone to look after the attempt at bee raising, which was a new item on the Carver agenda demanding attention. In November, 1898, friction began to arise in the agricultural department, of which the Iowa professor had charge, and complaints flowed into Booker's office saying that certain workmen were not treated fairly by the head of the department. The president wrote suggesting that Carver "treat one of the new assistants with respect due him."

This was the first of a series of complaints against the professor, which culminated in a half-dozen years with Carver's resignation from his teaching post.

During the year 1899 Carver faced a varied barrage of orders from the president which gives an idea of the types of problems he must solve. The first one is an order, coming on April 3, for him either to have the wheelwright fix the wagons or break up the bodies for kindling wood. This was followed by a deluge of commands "to see that all the wells are repaired and curbed," "buy fruit trees and set them out," "buy a Guernsey bull and improve the herd," "teach poultry, as Mrs. Washington suggests, to a large number of girls. I think it is a good lesson to teach our students how to make a simple beginning with whatever is right about them." "Whitewash the chicken house and keep it in an attractive condition."

He did these things as incidentals to the main course of his work, such as teaching regular classes to the students in agriculture, experimenting with soils, growing field crops in an endeavor to improve the quality, and beginning the investigations of crop types that would prove financially profitable to the

Alabama farmers, especially those of Macon County, where the Institute was located.

Carver, then about thirty-five, cut an attractive figure on the campus and about the fields as he went from farm to farm locating various types of clays and soils for his experimentations. His main problem was that of soil improvement, for the "soil was of a very poor quality, ranging from coarse sand to fine sandy loam and clay loam." Such crops as were raised on it matched in poorness the quality of the land. Hence his chief problem was that of building up the soil to make it profitably productive.

Although he did the best he could the first year, he showed a net loss of $16.25, which by the following year was built to a profit of $4. Year by year on the Institute's farm land he worked carefully with scientific fertilizers which he created, until in 1904 he produced eighty bushels of sweet potatoes per acre, and also grew another pay crop on the same land. This gave him a return of seventy-five dollars per acre. The following year this land produced a bale of cotton per acre. Thus he proved his contention that where the soil was properly cultivated, fertilized scientifically, and crops were selected in accordance to the soil-type, the land would be productive.

His main emphasis during the early years was to change the farmer's viewpoint regarding the type of crops to grow and to get the Negro away from the idea of a one-crop farm. He mingled with the farmers, visited their fields, spoke at their gatherings and gradually began to sell them on his ideas. Also he began to make a study of the farmer's diet, and taught them to substitute such foods as cow-peas, sweet potatoes and vegetables for the traditional corn bread and bacon. In his lectures to farm gatherings this was one of the outstanding topics for discussion.

This gradually gave him the name of being a "soil doctor," and his status in the farming communities began to rise until he was looked upon as a farm authority and soil scientist. Carver's attention was directed to problems of a different nature than those in which his chief, Dr. Washington, was immediately interested, and this often entangled him in difficulties, which within a few years came to a climax in the form of his resignation from the teaching staff.

The year 1900 saw his petty problems of production increased many fold, and along with his teaching and soil experimentation he had to terrace the home farm, look after the trees and grass, make the men cultivate close to the fences, enlarge the hog run, make money out of the poultry, — especially commanded — dig drain ditches, tear down the Gregory house, "an eyesore," plant velvet beans near the waste woods in the cow lot, care for the wagon bodies, whitewash hog pens where "the sows and their pigs are kept," and "cut the dead trees." Booker T. wrote, saying, "There should be some arrangement by which the harness will be regularly and systematically greased." He even had the task of overseeing the erection of hayracks in the horse and mule stalls.

This was the year in which the president began to insist that Carver become a productive poultry farmer, giving him an allowance of $150 to spend for ducks, chickens, geese and eggs. Those ducks later caused the president to remark, "You can't raise ducks," and he also found out that the professor in the chicken business was "long on theory and short on practice." The time came when the scientist's shortcomings were so evident that Washington demanded he sell the ducks immediately, even at a terrific loss.

By the end of the following year these details and insignificant-appearing—to Carver at least—duties were so demanding that the professor had little time for his real love of experimentation. He was so engrossed in supervising the trimming of trees, harvesting of hay, unstopping of sewers and buying a buggy "with a top" that his laboratory work was neglected.

Here were two mighty personalities beginning the inevitable clash with each other, each in his sphere supreme and famed in the end, but both as diverse in outlook as the poles are apart. Booker T. was an active man of productive ability, able to create that which he could measure in terms of new buildings, an enlarged endowment, increased enrollment. George W.'s ability lay in the opposite direction, and he cared little for the idea of jumboism. He was willing to work on a creative idea twenty years and when it was perfected put it away in the pigeon-holes of his head or file it in his cases, and do nothing at all about the results henceforth.

Washington's emphasis was always on "doing something about it," "making it pay its own way," "produce tangible and seeable results." The greatness of Carver's life is to be found in the other direction. After making his most revolutionary discoveries he was "too busy to patent them." Had he possessed the business acumen of his chief in the president's chair, he could have been one of America's wealthiest men.

But that was not his concern. He was a scientist for science's sake and cared nothing for the monetary returns from his discoveries. In later years it became a conviction with him that it was God's will for him not to charge for any service he performed, and he freely gave his most valuable discoveries and formulas to anyone who wrote requesting them.

In 1925 and 1927 somebody evidently prevailed upon him to patent a few of his discoveries, but nothing ever came of it. The things he patented were so insignificant in comparison with the more valuable products of his experimentation that the very idea of patenting them is ludicrous. For instance, on January 6, 1925, he patented his process for making cosmetics, face powders and creams from the peanut. Six months later he secured patents on his processes for manufacturing paints and stains, including cold water paints, from clays and minerals. Two years later he patented his Penol, a creosote emulsion from peanut juices.

Nothing ever came of such actions, for the greatness of his character was not in the manufacturing and distribution of his products. The quasi-psychiatric term *introvert* — which one hesitates to use because of its indefiniteness and lack of scientific discrimination in personality adjustments — would almost classify Dr. Carver. For the sheer love of discovery he spent his long years in the laboratory.

He was just as willing during those early 1900's to spend a week analyzing the soil of the poorest Negro farmer as he would have been to take an assignment which if followed up would have produced a hundred thousand dollars a year. He proved this in the end. There was never a time in his career when he arose above the status of being a poor-relative for the Southern farmer, Southern manufacturer, fruit grower, or Florida orange producer.

All of these kept his laboratory busy and stacked full of samples which they asked him to analyze, "okay," seal with his approval; and when through kindness they sent him a check for his services, whether it was of large or small amount, he always sent it back. When a commercial firm offered him a hundred thousand dollars a year to become their research scientist, he refused and his records of the very next week reveal that he examined a carload of hay gratis for some Macon County farmer! Even Edison's $175,000-a-year offer for his services was rejected. All the while he was busy asking the great Creator, "Why did you make the peanut? and what is it good for?"

As he wrote to Booker T. Washington, the giant-intellect man, he wanted to come to Tuskegee to be "of service to my people." Though at the time he was motivated by a desire soon to turn this farm work over to an assistant and devote his attention to his brush, still the thought of unselfish service never forsook him. For this reason he was never too busy to "examine a hog which I find in the storehouse, and I must pronounce it unfit for human consumption."

When a neighbor's chickens died, he took time to perform an autopsy, and his pronouncement was: "Death caused by eating ice cream salt." He was never rushed in these humble services, and while to him they appeared on the surface as time-wasters, still to his neighbors, the white farmers, the Negro tenants, he felt they were supremely important. Hence his time was at their service.

During these early years of the 1900's it became more and more evident that Carver's ability was to be found in some sphere other than making the Institute farm a paying proposition. Under him was an assistant who had the knack of being a productive farmer, and while Dr. Carver was experimenting, this assistant, Bridgeforth, was able to go into the fields and get results. This evidently "went to his head," and he became insulting to Carver, chief of the agriculture department.

The arguments went back and forth until on December 3, 1904, the plant doctor wrote a long letter of accusation to his assistant, saying, "I do not like your attitude, neither do I like the position you have taken and maintained for some weeks. It has been and is very unsatisfactory to me and of course cannot continue . . . I have no objection to your taking up any matter with the principal (Booker T.). But there are certain courtesies which I demand, and will have, if the persons stay in my employ. I want it clearly understood that I am not going to put up with such notes as this coming into my office from you."

All this discussion arose concerning the number of teams Bridgeforth was to use in his farm work. On the sixth, the assistant replied to the head of the department. "Your notes," he wrote " . . . are in every respect laughable . . . I can hardly see how any educated man could put such interpretation on a plain outspoken letter . . . I shall not stand another bit of this bluff and you must do business like a man and take some interest . . . You seem to have lost all interest in things at the school . . . I am not to be intimidated by your recent threats . . . "

This was a plain letter, in which the assistant "pulled no punches," but the good professor, knowing more about plant chemistry than human psychological reactions, pressed the matter further, until ultimately he appealed to Dr. Washington to settle the argument. By December 14, Booker T. was in Washington, D.C. and replied to Carver's note thus:

"It requires a higher degree of ability, often, to correct the weak points in an assistant and cause him to work in harmony than to get rid of him. I believe that a good frank talk between you two would in a large degree straighten out the tangle. I require all under you to obey and respect your authority . . ."

He appended a line saying that it was better for the heads of departments to straighten out the tangles than for the principal to be forced to do so for them.

Here was a personality which Carver never seemed to be able to handle strategically. Though the local incidents were usually smoothed over satisfactorily, in the end Bridgeforth was able to gain the president's ear, and the time came when Booker T. placed Carver in an underling position to Bridgeforth. This brought the inevitable clash, and Carver was ready to move to St. Louis. We shall say more about this later.

It seemed that the wizard was so engrossed with his scientific investigations, chemical analyses of soils, and diagnoses of plant and animal diseases he had little time for assistants. All of these clashes between Carver and Bridgeforth and often between him and Booker T. contributed toward the result which gave Carver his great field.

A man of his ability had no business trying to meet Booker's demand, which he stated on November 30, 1905, for "vigorous chicken and egg production for spring." Nor should he have been forced to write the chief a letter, as he did five weeks later, asking for "another work animal for the farm." Matters like these were incidentals and should have been left entirely to such men as Bridgeforth, whose forte they proved to be.

God wanted Carver for one thing — plant investigation, a scientific study of the South's agricultural problems; not from the standpoint of production but for the purpose of trail blazing, pointing the way to better methods of crop improvement. And it was not until Booker Washington put Bridgeforth at the head of the department and made Carver an experiment specialist that he was shunted in the direction where his main contribution to agricultural chemistry was to be found.

Washington, wanting results which Carver could not produce, said in substance, "Let a man have the job who can, and you can tinker with test tubes all you please." When the professor, six or more years later, got where he could see this, then he really began his great contribution to the South and to his race.

In spite of Booker's demand for chickens, the scientist in the professor drove his interest to the sweet potato, which was his "first love." The peanut was to come later. While at Tuskegee early in 1943, I asked when the good plant wizard became interested in the peanut, and I always received this answer: "From the beginning." But his works do not show this to be true. His first love was the sweet potato, which during his earliest years he thought held one of the answers to the South's problem of production, being scientifically geared to catch the financial eyes of the nation.

On November 29, 1905, he sent the chief two sweet

potatoes which had been dug early in September, saying they had been preserved in the basement, and "for six years I have been experimenting with keeping sweet potatoes in this manner." He urged the doctor to visit his demonstration on the nine ways to cook the sweet potato. "The exhibit consists of 185 jars and I am still putting up different samples."

He never lost this keen sense of increasing the South's ability to feed itself, always being busy with some experiment, for instance, pickling pork chops so they will "keep three years," methods of canning wild plums, of which that section possesses an abundance, the use of cow-peas, and similar items.

His attention also was directed to another interest which time and again appears in his work. While Carver was supremely a plant doctor, he also was an expert in the treatment of animal diseases. It took Booker T. a long time to be persuaded of this, but in the end he came to look upon the scientist as a "top doctor." Early in 1905 the Institute hogs died in great numbers and Carver analyzed the situation as "cough, weak appearance, crowding in the pens, watering eyes. Chief needs: shelter, removal of dead and medication. I shall be glad to suspend every thing and fix up a quantity of medicine." By February 25 he wrote that the dead hogs reached the number of 189, "with eight dead last night."

When the experimenter turned his attention to the difficulty he did it with scientific thoroughness and shortly there were no more dead hogs reported. This brings to mind the story which Dr. F. D. Patterson, at present president of Tuskegee Institute, told me of his early relationship with the famous ebony wizard.

"When I first came here," President Patterson related, as we sat in his office at the Institute, facing a life-sized painting of Dr. Carver, who had died less than a month previous, "I was the Institute veterinary. Farmers reported that their hogs were dying of some unknown malady, and I could not find the cause. So I asked Dr. Carver to go with me and together we made a thorough investigation of every form of food the animals had been eating. An autopsy of their stomachs revealed the presence of a poison which ate away the lining.

"Dr. Carver checked every possible clue, and in the end found the cause to be the root of the polk berry, which bore a deadly poison. When the doctor was through with his experimentation there were no more poisoned hogs."

This is but one of the many examples of the thoroughness with which Carver worked when faced by a problem of importance to the farmers of the South.

The years of 1905 and 1906 were busy ones for him, since Dr. Washington constantly threw into his hands some new issue, such as a request made October 14, 1905, that the dairy herd be investigated and a complete report be made regarding the condition.

His report is interesting for its thoroughness and for its recommendation: (1) Pasture condition good. (2) Some cows give only small amount of milk. (3) Cut food green and moldy which lowers its feeding capacity. (4) Cow grooming not carefully and thoroughly done. (5) Lack of personal supervision. Recommendations: (1) Weed out the herd. (2) Feed cattle better. (3) Groom the cows systematically. (4) Milk the cows clean "and strip them."

For some time previous Dr. Washington had been

toying with the idea of an "experiment wagon" which could be used to carry Carver's results from one farm community to another. Accordingly, just before 1905 began Dr. Carver worked out a rough sketch of such a wagon, which had a detachable top that could be removed when not traveling, and thus the vehicle could double for an ordinary farm wagon.

"It should be supplied with large charts," he said, "on soil building, orcharding, stock raising, feeding charts and all operations pertaining to the farm . . . "

When Dr. Washington read the letter and checked the sketch, he scrawled on it, "Drawing shows no dimensions, details or anything." Of course, those were matters in the scientist's head. He was engrossed with the idea and the details to him were insignificant. In the end the plan prevailed and such a wagon was outfitted for "exhibition tours" through the neighboring sections of the country.

This was to give a new slant to the scientist's interests and activities. Until now he had been more or less localized in his effort, and, while at Ames he had spoken at agricultural and botanical conferences, conventions and the like, his Tuskegee contacts had been limited to the Institute group and neighboring farms.

This new venture was to take him far afield, and before two decades should pass, he was destined to carry his message to a large part of the nation through his own personal appearances. Had he done nothing else than this, as a goodwill engineer he did much to create a helpful and happy feeling between his and the white race. There were to be few places in the nation where he, as a Negro, was not welcomed. In the South this was particularly true. In that land where the Negro's status is not so high as in the North, there was as wide-open a door for Carver's entrance as for any white scientist, educator, or speaker.

That first roughly sketched wagon, to which Booker T. objected because the drawings were not complete, was the root from which sprang his marvelous career as a goodwill harbinger. Carver by this time had found himself, and had begun to experiment with the ideas which later were to make him famous. As yet he had attained only local recognition, but the foundation had been laid and his future worth to society was assured.

Immediately Carver began gathering groups of farmers at schoolhouses where he exhibited his products, showing his method of improving soils, increasing crop output and demonstrating to the women better canning procedures. He made a report to the president on November 28, 1905, stating the number of trips he had made and the total number of people present. This showed that he had spoken at Liberty Hill, 300 present; at Big Swamp, 212 present; at Magnolia, 200 present. The total number of trips he listed at seven with many people in attendance.

While he was still very closely tied to the Institute grounds and farm, and his duties increased amazingly fast, he was beginning to gain such a reputation that he was called to address farm groups far and near. He had told Booker T., "I want to get in touch with as many white and colored farmers as possible in Alabama and Georgia," and to this end he bent his efforts. His trips in 1906 were interspersed with such labors as "killing the rats in the chicken pens," cleaning after the Short Termers' mules which littered the grounds back of the agriculture building, producing eggs at a too-small rate to suit Washington, planning a feeding campaign for the college hogs, and the usual grind of classes which he taught.

In May, 1906, he went to the Farmers' Conference, held at Tallahassee, Florida, where he gave advice on such topics as rental systems, buying lands, how to diversify crops, and rural schools and rural homes, which indeed showed the diversity of his interests. "A splendid barbecued dinner followed the session and all went away pleased," he notes, "pledging themselves to act as missionaries to bring in more next year."

Shortly again he was the speaker at the Walker Baptist Institute, and the bulletin sent out to the farmers declared that Dr. Carver "wants you to bring samples of your crops," and the church added the note, "Let each one bring a dollar to defray the expenses." These visits increased as the story of his fame spread among the farmers of the vicinity. At Pensacola, July 30, of that year, he states, "I visited two churches on Sunday and spoke for an hour and a half Monday night to representative people, strictly on agriculture."

During the years from 1906 until 1910 there was an increasing friction between Booker T. and the professor. Dr. Washington carefully checked Carver's reports, and in each one he would note some lack, which usually centered around a failure to produce enough eggs, hatch sufficient chickens or the poor "showing the geese were making." On the surface these were insignificant in comparison with the larger things which the professor was achieving. For instance, in making his ten-year report in 1906, he indicated what he had done since arriving at the Institute.

In 1896-97, he made ninety-seven experiments with sweet potatoes, on sixteen well-selected plots of ground. Likewise he performed ninety-eight with cow-peas, velvet beans and corn for forage purposes. In another ninety-nine experiments thirteen varieties of cotton were planted, fertilized and cultivated and the results tabulated; in the same way and a similar number of times he worked with sorghum.

From 1900-05, he studied sorghum; Red Fulsum wheat, producing thirty-five bushels per acre; rye, twenty-four bushels; barley, twenty bushels — all of which were tested for "cover crop, grazing and yield per acre." In 1903 he experimented with the Irish potato, but noted that his success was nothing phenomenal. The following year he planted nine varieties of cotton, and records "fine results on cotton." His first vital reference to the peanut comes in this report when he says that in 1905 he grew fifty bushels of peanuts per acre.

This report was given in written form to the principal, but the records reveal no particular interest on the president's part. From 1907 until 1910 there is a growing reference in Booker's correspondence with Carver to the "poultry situation," as he terms it. For instance, on April 15, 1908, Booker was in New York City and after checking one of Carver's reports, he wrote saying that in his own private yard there were almost a fourth as many chickens as Carver had at the Experiment Station. "Unless you can do better, the matter is going to prove very expensive," declared Washington.

Five days later came a note from New York City,

"I do not understand about ducks. It seems that we have only eighteen ducks. What is the trouble?"

The next year these egg-tirades flowed into Carver's office from wherever the president happened to be. One read, "Very small quantity of eggs in incubators for this season. Think should be kept full." By June 14, 1910, the president could no longer stand the geese situation, and he wrote, "You do not seem to be carrying out my order very vigorously to get rid of the geese." He even went so far as to send Dr. Carver a night letter from New York City, "Very important you do something immediately to stop death rate among chickens."

Despite the excellent results produced by the professor in every other field of endeavor, chickens seemed to be the bone of contention between him and the president. Ostensibly this was the point of clash, but after going through the hundreds of letters as they flew back and forth between the two, now filed in the Department of Records and Research, I was not satisfied that the whole story had been placed on paper. So I went out to the little cemetery, just beyond the Institute Chapel, where Dr. Washington's grave is, and where but recently they had laid George Washington Carver to rest.

Here, as he was performing a service of love, I discovered D. A. Williston, long Dr. Carver's friend and a famous landscape architect whose services are in demand by the government at Washington, and sitting on a little marble slab, he started telling me the story, which had never been placed in print.

"Chickens were only a minor and insignificant part of it," he said. "You read his letters where he resigned in 1910?" he asked, and before I could reply, he went on, resting his chin in the cup of his right hand, as he waved with his left to the workmen to indicate that they should build higher the mound around Dr. Carver's grave, which he was landscaping, "Well, you see it is like this." However, before he could finish the story, a car drove up, and with little or no ceremony, he said, "Five o'clock. I'll see you tomorrow," and was gone.

HIS DISCOVERIES A DIVINE REVELATION . . .

"My discoveries come like a divine revelation from God. The idea and the method of working out a new product come all together . . .

"In half an hour after the idea was revealed to me, I produced the yolk of an egg from the Puerto Rico sweet potato . . .

"Anything will give up its secrets, if you love it enough."

—Spoken by Dr. Carver to the Woman's Board of Domestic Missions of the Reformed Church, Marble Collegiate Church, New York City

CHAPTER V

GROWING RECOGNITION

The climax had been reached. For several years the Professor had gradually shown his inability to produce sufficient marketable products to make his department a financial success. In reality he had been little concerned over this phase of his work. To him the important things were not chickens and eggs, ducks and geese, huge outputs of hogs and cotton, hay and peanuts, but a scientifically directed experimental study of the more intricate problems related to crop improvement. And to this end he marshaled his mind forces.

He could look after egg production, but he was more enticed with the thoughts of making eggs out of the Puerto Rican sweet potato than doubling egg production. These things he wanted to leave for others to accomplish. Until now he had been driven to externalities by that powerful personality sitting in the president's office, and had little time for the field in which his genius was to find its full stature.

But genius cannot be forced into narrow bounds, nor congealed in forms dictated by official strategy. As Dean Thompson of Howard University, doubtless the nation's outstanding authority on Booker T. Washington, aptly said to the author some weeks ago, "Booker T. modeled his life on the standard of the captains of industry, the great industrial geniuses of his generation, and he was a man who said, 'Do this,' and expected his word to be law as well as the final court of appeal."

However, Carver's genius could not be dictated to; so the president demanded a reorganization of the department of which the Iowa professor was head. The man who built Tuskegee into the famous institution it now is could tolerate nothing which interfered with making his dream come true. So on November 16, 1910, he sent Professor Carver the plan for the reorganization of the department, in which he outlined the doctor's duties. Henceforth Carver was to be in charge of the Experiment Station, to supervise the creation and distribution of publications, such as the bulletins he had already published, and was to give attention to the experimental examination of foods.

Thus far Carver was perfectly satisfied with the plan and in accord with the demands. It was the second condition which struck him a bitter blow. In the new scheme, Bridgeforth, the production man, was to have charge of the department of agriculture, with Carver serving as dean under him. Likewise Bridgeforth was to direct teaching arrangements, and the professor was to be his assistant. The scope of work which the plant doctor was to have under Bridgeforth was to be large enough to keep his talents directly invested in his chosen field, but the spirit of the man was wounded. A study of the Booker-T.-and-George-W. correspondence over a half-dozen years indicates that at the basis of these demands was the poultry business.

"This arrangement puts also the poultry yard under Mr. Bridgeforth," Booker T. said in his letter to the professor. " . . . In carrying out this plan . . . Mr. Carver is to have the fullest scope for making original research and doing whatever independent work he may think best not inconsistent with the orders of Mr. Bridgeforth."

The president, in checking the use of Experiment Station land, had found that much of it lay idle most of the year, and Bridgeforth had been producing three crops a year to Carver's one. In a previous note to the professor, Dr. Washington had told him as much.

At once the plant doctor felt his dignity had been injured, and the arrangement was unsatisfactory to him. The first part was ideal, but the thought of working under Bridgeforth galled his spirit, and so he sent his resignation to the president.

"As this means the best thing to do," he wrote to Booker T. on November 19, "I beg of you to carry it out, but I cannot be honest with you and true to the course for which I have given nearly fifteen years of the best of my life. So therefore I tender my resignation to take effect as soon as my work can be put in order and the department inventorial work is over. I trust that the work will grow and prosper as never before, and I shall always be grateful to you for your past favors. I am yours truly, Geo. W. Carver."

This was a hard step to take, for there were many unfinished pieces of research which he did not like to abandon. For instance, he had been working on the Carver Hybrid Prolific Cotton, and many excellent reports had been coming to him, such as the following, a letter dated September 16, 1910:

"The Carver Hybrid Prolific Cotton is the best-looking cotton in south Baldwin County."

Also on the day following the receipt of this letter Carver sent a note to the president saying that the

German government wanted his recommendation as to the best cotton to grow in their African colonies. There were sweet-potato plots, peanut experiments, and a dozen other items on the agenda of his research work which demanded finishing. He faced the problem, if he resigned, of finding a new teaching post where these researches could be brought to fruition. He did not lack offers of teaching posts, for they had been many, and one was particularly enticing to him. A St. Louis school was calling vociferously for his services, since his bulletins, which we shall note later, had attracted widespread attention . . .

While I was waiting for tomorrow to come so that friend Williston could give me the inside information on this resignation, I reread the correspondence, mentally noting the shock this step had given the professor. I met the landscape architect the next afternoon, and as we stood over the departed scientist's grave, he unraveled the story that had not been written.

"For a long time," he said, taking up the account where he left it the evening previous, "Bridgeforth had been howling in Washington's ears . . . God bless his memory . . . " — pointing to the president's grave just a few steps from us and the towering evergreens which marked its site — "that there ought to be more students in the department studying agriculture, and he assured Booker T. that if the president would just give him charge of the department he could fill it with students."

"And Washington listened to the story?" I asked.

Nodding assent, he went on, "When Washington made Bridgeforth head of the department over Carver, that was one thing George could not stand, so he resigned. When I heard about it, I went to my friend and asked him what he wanted to do. He said, 'I'm going to accept the job in St. Louis.' I countered, 'But don't you think it would be better to stay here and let Booker give you a department of research all to yourself?'

"It was a new thought to George W. and I went to Booker T. telling him that Carver was going to leave unless something happened. Said the president, 'Oh, he'll swell up for a while, but in the end he'll stay with Tuskegee.' When I assured him that the professor was sincere in his resignation, I suggested that a new department of research be created, where George could be absolutely free to do the experimenting he wanted to and Bridgeforth could have charge of the production end as the new plan called for."

"Do you think Carver would stay with us if we created the research department for him?" asked the president.

On being assured by Williston that he would, Washington said, "I'll create the department of agricultural research and Professor Carver shall have entire charge of it."

Thus Williston brought Booker T. and George W. together in their thoughts and intent, and two days later a committee was appointed which made the recommendations resulting in the new work for the plant wizard. These included: (1) Establishment of a department of research headed by Carver, assisted by a consultant; also an Experiment Station to publish bulletins on bacteriological work, analysis of soils, water, milk, food for human and stock consumption, paints, and oils. Likewise there was to be an extension department to sponsor agriculture lectures, domestic science and poultry yards.

(2) A first-class laboratory was to be established in which Carver could conduct investigations "he may wish to undertake along the lines mentioned."

(3) This department was to be independent of all others, subject only to the restrictions which the president should place upon it.

A note was appended which said, "He may teach agriculture classes if he desires."

Standing by the scientist's last resting place, Williston said, "Often through the years Professor Carver thanked me for my help at that time in keeping him here. Just last summer he said, 'I can never be grateful enough for what you did to keep me at Tuskegee and really to help me get into the type of work where I have done the most good.' "

It was this seeming detour in his life's road which gave George W. his real opportunity. The new laboratory was to become the throne from which his influence was to touch all corners of American life. Nor was he long in launching into his research. He was impatient with the committee for not setting up the experiment center and equipping it so rapidly as he desired. He seemed to think that the magical pressing of a button would produce the facilities for the intricate experiments he planned.

But when the laboratory was ready for him, he was most grateful, saying on September 11, 1911, "I am perfectly safe in saying that you" — speaking to Dr. Washington — "will not regret having equipped this place for high-class work. If I can get the materials in a short time I will show you things about the clays that will save the school hundreds, possibly thousands, of dollars per year, besides bringing the reputation to the institution and to Negro education that nothing else has done up to date."

This was a prophecy destined in the years to come true — not only in respect to the school's reputation but its financial aspect as well.

During the summer it was not an uncommon sight to see the dignified professor walking the clay roads of the Tuskegee vicinity searching for unusually colored clays, samples of which he would gather, and on returning to the laboratory, send through the various stages of the process whereby he tested them for colors. Many of these samples emerged from this color-testing process with the most delicate tints possible. Clay at this time was prominent in his range of interests, and it was this enthusiasm which finally produced the marvelous paints and stains for which he became famous.

On July 19, Carver sent word to the principal that he had gone into the country to see a house which a certain Mrs. Pugh had whitewashed with clay. He noted later that she had mixed the clay with water and without the use of lime had obtained an attractive color. By adding bluing to the mixture, "she got a paint or stain which she used for a picture frame." On finding the clays similar to a deposit at Tuskegee, Carver became rhapsodic over its potentialities.

"I feel sure that none of us except yourself," writing again to the principal, "has the slightest idea as to the great number of uses to which this clay in its many varieties can be put . . . I have one out of which I have made a beautiful black color by simply mixing a small amount of boiler black with it . . . which is equivalent to lamp black. Black used in paint is simply some form of carbon, charcoal, with the proper oils mixed with it. Now, with the great amount of coal we burn here, and the amount of soot that we could collect from our boilers, it would pay us to save this instead of throwing it away . . .

"Just as soon as I get into my laboratory I will make up all these things for you . . . The more I work with it the more enthusiastic I am."

This was not only a promissory enthusiasm, but it was turned into actual results, as his labors have shown. Before the fall term arrived he had made face powder from clay, samples of which he sent to the principal and others who were interested, asking them to "give it to your friends." This phase of his clay work has progressed to such an extent that within the past two or three years the Carvoline Company has been formed, which promotes a very excellent type of face lotions, known as the Ermine Lotion. This company is the only business venture to which Dr. Carver has given his sanction and which he has permitted to use his name.

Before the fall term of 1911 opened the professor was to have trouble with an assistant, A. L. Evans, for although the Research Laboratory had been set up, Carver still had duties related to the department of agriculture, even bearing some of the hated poultry responsibility. As always, Booker T. charged him with "not knowing how to raise ducks . . . He (Evans) can't stand the constant nagging from you." Evans, however, stayed with the department, and the good professor, to show that he was happy in the prospect of his research labors, was perfectly willing to "replace at my own expense" the chickens lost in the recent exhibition.

Before the year was out, the research scientist proved that he was able to master the poultry business, even to the principal's satisfaction, and Booker wrote him from the East saying, "Congratulate you . . . on your success in raising poultry. We have now on hand the largest number in the history of the school." Once poultry raising was mastered, Carver was ready to turn his attention to worthier and heavier matters than furnishing the president (and his faculty) with the makings of "good ole Southern brown-fried chicken."

Early in the summer Washington asked Carver to send a photograph of himself to the Doubleday, Page and Company, who were publishing the president's *My Larger Education*, which, when it appeared late in December, 1911, caused Carver to write Booker's secretary, saying:

" . . . and in looking through it I was dumbfounded to see such an elaborate write-up. Had I known what was going on I certainly would have protested. I prefer to work quietly, doing my duty accurately as nearly as I can and as God gives me light. Mr. Washington in his great heart has placed a tremendous responsibility on me, which I shall endeavor to not only maintain but further develop . . . Leaving out the Personal I consider this one of the most interesting of all his books. I predict a large sale for it."

When I discovered the letter in the old files, I read it to Dr. Monroe Work, long a Carver associate, and Dean Thompson of Howard, an authority on Washington. Dr. Work remarked, apropos of the letter's sentiment, "He really was glad his story was there, for he enjoyed publicity," to which Dean Thompson added, "The letter was prompted by his becoming modesty."

It is evident, however, that the new plan for the expensive laboratory was not meeting with the greatest of success, for a council was called in the president's office to discuss the matter, and Carver, after hearing the remarks, said, "I was not pleased with the turn of events in your office yesterday. The new department is not going to receive sympathy . . . "

Later Booker T. thought it necessary to set the professor straight on a matter of policy; so he wrote:

"We cannot stand any further or pursue a policy which permits you or anyone else to argue at length every order that is given, and to lay down the conditions upon which you will work . . . You have had charge of the experiment station for some twelve or fifteen years . . . The rule has been to leave you in absolute control . . . This year the school has thought it wise to give you a definite order. Instead of complying with this order in a sympathetic and prompt manner you are dillydallying with it, and have tried in many ways to bring influence to bear . . . to get us to change this order. This is not the proper way to act . . . you lose influence and power by such actions . . .

"There are few people anywhere who have greater ability to inspire and instruct . . . When it comes to organizing classes . . . you are wanting in ability. When it comes to the matter of practical farm managing . . . you are wanting in ability . . . It is a rare individual who combines all the elements of success . . .

"You have great ability in original research . . . I was greatly surprised to find that you wish a laboratory fitted for your exclusive use and that you do not mean to give instruction to any student in this laboratory . . .

"I am simply trying to say that we have now reached the point where you will have to decide whether you intend to do the thing the school wants done or . . . stick to a policy of doing what you want to do . . . "

This letter produced the results Booker T. desired, and on the following day the professor wrote saying that he was willing to comply, " . . . I am perfectly willing to make out a course of instruction and teach . . . but cannot adjust myself to anything that brings me under Mr. Bridgeforth."

One remark is prominent among the comments made by those who knew Professor Carver the longest: "He never spoke an unkind word about anybody." And in all his letters, this difficulty with Bridgeforth is the nearest I found to a lack of personality adjustment to any individual. Henceforth there are to be found no other untoward remarks concerning Bridgeforth, and the clash of wills between Carver and Dr. Washington here reaches its end.

March, 1912, furnished a practical demonstration of Carver's ability to gear his research work to definite results. He had been experimenting with paints made from native clays, and on March 25, he informed the president that the new Episcopal Church in the town of Tuskegee was painting the woodwork with stains made from Macon County clays. "I am keeping a very close eye on this work . . . In color it is an exquisite shade of dark mission . . . called weathered oak and antique finish."

He also said it had been tested along with paints

costing three dollars a gallon, and "I was able to make this stain for one-tenth of that amount . . . I am working out others as fast as possible."

This first demonstration of his paints and stains attracted the attention of the Fitzpatrick Drug Company in Arkansas, which asked for details regarding his use of clays in oil and water, especially "on ochres, browns, reds and other colors," he had developed. By the middle of July, 1912, he circularized the president and others, saying that these paints and stains could be furnished at seventy-five cents a gallon in "Florentine brown, light sienna, dark sienna, light mahogany."

He added another achievement to his list by making a soldering fluid from native products, "which can be furnished on short notice to anyone wanting the same." Though Booker T. could not see the advantage of furnishing him with a laboratory to be used solely by himself, Carver began to furnish the doctor with practical demonstrations in terms of money saved. On August 1, the president was informed by the soil chemist that he had developed a soil fertilizer, concerning which it was "impossible to estimate in dollars its value in permanently building up the soil . . . " Washington could understand that language, and henceforth the research scientist was given the go-sign and the laboratory began to produce tangible results.

A local house was painted with the stain made from clay for the first time on August 7, when Carver visited Moses Harris "to get him started off on his painting." Just before the fall term opened that year, Carver announced a powder that he had made from clay, a powder which could be used for cleaning silver, and on submitting samples to the president, he said, "I would appreciate it if you will let me know how you like it."

When the Institute cotton crop was harvested, and Carver had an opportunity to measure the results of his soil-building fertilization and the efficacy of his own hybrid-seed, he informed the office that he had raised a bale and three-fourths from one and one-fifth acres, but he suggested, "I think the effect will be better if you leave my name off of this report sent to the farms, as the management resents it."

The year the first World War opened Carver proved his practical worth by developing a dust to kill the Colorado beetle on white potatoes, saying when he presented it to the administration, "One dusting was made . . . and today practically every bug is dead." On the same day, May 1, he circularized those in charge of the buildings that he had made a bedbug exterminator. "As to killing the bugs, all I ask is that you give it a chance." He went on to remark that he had left out the perfumery, "which is rather costly, but as far as killing the bugs is concerned it will kill them just as well." When the president's office heard of the results, a hundred gallons for Institute use were ordered at a "savings of fourteen dollars." Remarked the lady who used it, " . . . not only kills the bugs but does not stain."

When the guest house, Dorthy Hall, was built, Carver informed Dr. Washington that "the walls were kalsomined with native clay. The woodwork is stained with stains made from native clay, and the windows are painted with paints made from native clay." For the new teachers' dining room many gallons of a cherry-colored kalsomine and sienna paint were prepared in the scientist's laboratory. Toward the end of the year, when asked for one hundred gallons of pink, yellow, gray and buff kalsomines for the academic buildings and the new cottages, Carver remarked that "all the colors will be taken from a ditch near Tompkins Hall."

Standing recently back of the Tompkins Hall, I looked into the ditch where the genius — this artist — had gathered the clays for his colors and his stains. Only a wizard, who is directed by some higher sense or power could extract the rainbow colors from those Alabama clays which for centuries had gone unused.

War conditions produced a strain in the Institute's budget and a finance committee on the revamping rampage suggested that the scientist lay off for one month during the summer of 1914, but when news of this decision came to the professor as he was busy in his laboratory, at once he reacted very violently.

"To this I do not agree," he said to the committee, whose report had been sanctioned by Dr. Washington, "because it is not a question of salary. I saved the school last year in the months of June, July, August to September 1, $399, by manufacturing things it would have had to pay a much higher price for."

He went on to remark that it was too much trouble to look elsewhere for work during the one month. "Of course if the school has reached the point where it cannot pay me and doesn't need my services anymore, I shall abide by the decision."

He asked for a quick decision on the part of the administration, and when the answer came from Dr. Washington — an answer not altogether satisfactory to the professor — he responded, "I have been here nearly eighteen years . . . I have been working for the same salary that I came here on; I never asked for a cent more . . . I have taken only one vacation of the allotted ten days since coming . . .

"I have worked with the hope and feeling that, when my head begins to silver over as it is now, I would have a home. I am not clamoring for more dollars, but this forces me to seek a place where I can have some assurance of being cared for when I reach the point where I am not so vigorous as I am now."

As one looks back upon this letter from thirty years later, when Doctor Carver had attained the full measure of his fame, and had even to the eighty mark worked quietly in his laboratory with a free and unconstrained hand, the worry seems needless. For many years after that first World War, the scientist was a revered figure around the Institute, which gave him what he wanted: a sphere of influence, a laboratory for research, food and shelter and gentle hands to care for his needs and in the end to perform the rite connected with laying him away.

During these years when he was "on-the-make," to use a term in common parlance, his mind was never at rest. One day he worked out a system whereby the commissary expenses of the Institute could be reduced by the use of sweet potatoes and cow-peas in a dozen different ways, some of which were sweet potato cobbler, sweet potato pie, boiled peas with bacon, peas with pork, bacon fritters and sweet potatoes. The next day we find him writing, "I have made fifty-three different things from the feathers of domestic fowls, and have hardly begun to show their wonderful possibilities."

With amazing alacrity he leaped from one task to

another. For example, to help a friend, he tested clay for paint possibilities, then made from furnace ashes a lice killer for use on chickens, and thence, on February 13, 1915, undertook an experiment in which he fed cattle on chinaberries — and proved that cattle thus fed made satisfactory gains in weight.

It was merely a turn in his mental road to send a note to Booker T. that his alfalfa crop was ready for the president's cows to graze, and with a flip of his keen mind he could produce the following month, July 13, "a diet of twenty-one meals for farmers." By August he had weighed in the silage per acre from his corn crop and found it to be nine tons, "as well as forty bushels per acre."

This was the versatile genius who until now had been somewhat of a problem boy in the president's estimation, whose influence had been localized, and who in spite of his bulletins, produced on many subjects, did little else than create a favorable stir in the waters which were Tuskegee. He had only been laying his foundation, preparing himself thoroughly in scientific investigation, walking through the doors of truth which his own hands and those of God opened to him. His keen mind was ever alert to possibilities to increase the farmers' sources of income. He had but opened the gates to the golden opportunities which were to be his.

When the stressful years of the boll weevil, from 1912 to 1915 and '16, struck the South, Carver's fertile brain began to search for a cotton substitute as a cash crop, and out of this came the peanut industry. As the war days proved strenuous for the poor man's budget, Carver went to the laboratory and sought for a flour substitute, so that there might be enough flour for the United States and her allies, and he came out with a sweet potato flour, and in 1918 he went to Washington to persuade the government to provide driers for the sweet potato as a substitute for wheat flour.

"We haven't a single crop that will produce as many bushels per acre as the sweet potato," he said to the Ninth Annual Session of the Farmers' Conference at Denmark, South Carolina, in an address dealing with the sweet potato.

Two days earlier, speaking at the Voorhees Normal and Industrial School, of the same city, he said:

" . . . I deem it fitting for me to remind you again . . . to get one of the greatest of all gifts, wisdom; but best of all is to get wisdom and understanding, so beautifully outlined in the Book of books for our guidance. Science is simply the truth, that is all."

During the address he showed samples of his products, such as substitute pea breakfast food, substitute coffee, instant coffee and similar items which were of interest to every student and farmer.

The following week at the Tuskegee Farmers' Conference, he gave a complete demonstration of the many new products which he had made from the ordinary materials at hand. Some of these were: potash from chinaberry ashes; chinaberry meal; tonic stock feed, from velvet beans, cotton seed and chinaberries; dehydrated lye hominy; okra fiber made into paper, rope, strawboard, matting and carpets; ultramarine dyes for cotton, silk and wool, made from clays; poplar bark made into artificial ribbon; dyes from dandelions, black oak, wood ashes, sweet gum, swamp maples, pomegranates, peanuts, muscadine grapes, onions, tomato vines; shoe dressings made from clays;

scouring powders; white and color washes from clays; feathers made into many fancy items; and twenty types of laundry bluings made from various farm products.

Here we see the professor, long hidden in his laboratory, now ready to take his results to the public. Henceforth wherever he went his samples of farm products transformed into hundreds of wares were to go with him. He became literally a traveling exhibition of the chemist's use of those things which every farm in the South found near at hand.

"I believe . . . that America is on the eve of the greatest scientific development it has ever known," he said later in the year, "and is destined to become leaders rather than followers along many lines of practical endeavors . . . The chemist will no longer be satisfied to be a mere analyst . . . The ideal chemist of the future will be an investigator, one who dares to think independently, and unfolds before your eyes a veritable mystic maze of new and useful products."

This was a prophecy which we have seen fulfilled during the past twenty-five years. In the same speech he told of the magical results of his own work in plant chemistry, saying that from clay he had produced every hue in the color scale and had obtained beautiful and useful sienna and practical kalsomines in a wide range of tints.

He also pointed to the fact that he had discovered two hundred and fifty medicinal plants on the useful list of the South. Testifying to the practical turn of his mind during the years when the World War shut off the flow of German dyes to this country, he said that he had found a hundred well-selected dye plants, trees, herbs, flowers and barks which could be used to advantage at a moment's notice.

His first personal triumph came early in 1921 when the Ways and Means Committee of the United States Senate, at the insistence of the peanut lobbyists, sent for him to appear before them in behalf of the Hawley-Smoot Tariff Bill. This was an officious occasion for the professor, but he took it in his humble stride. Out of him had gone much of the youthful swagger which once marked his attitude toward public appearances. Nearing the sixty mark, he stood slightly stooped, but was regal in his bearing. The silver about which he had told Booker T. ten years earlier now had frosted his hair.

He was not the most tidy man in dress at this time of his life. His clothes were old, but clean and neatly pressed by his own iron, that is, when he left Tuskegee for Washington. When his friend suggested an addition to his wardrobe in the form of a new tie, the doctor — doctor in ability at least though the degree was not officially bestowed upon him until eight years later — shook his white-touched head and indicated that it would take more than a new tie to enable him to answer their questions.

On arriving at the Capital, he carried his exhibition box, filled with the magical elements which in the laboratory he had brewed from the humble peanut. Being a stranger in the city, he hailed a redcap and asked the way to the Senate building.

"Sorry, Pop, I ain't got time to tell you now," said the porter, "I'm lookin' for a great scientist on this train comin' from Alabama."

"Pop," as the colored porter had called Carver, picked up his box and made his way unaided to the

LEONARD M. JOHNSON

Senate. On arriving, he entered the room, sat at the back, and listened as a dozen or more other speakers presented their points in favor of and against the tariff. As his name was called, he untangled himself from the chair, lifted the box, and started to the front as a giggle ruffled the surface of the sedate Senators.

"What do you know about the tariff, old fellow?" asked a Senator, to be answered by the professor's quick wit, "I don't know much, but I know it's the thing that shuts the other fellow out."

This "broke the ice," and pulling out his dollar watch, he did not even take time to straighten the homemade necktie, but launched at once into his ten-minute speech. Through the maze of his peanut products he took these men, and when the ten minutes were up, they shouted for him to go on. For the next hour and thirty-five minutes his magical box spoke for itself. Out of it he drew face powder, axle grease, printer's ink, milk, cream, butter, shampoos, creosote, vinegar, coffee, soaps, salads, wood stains, oil dyes, breakfast foods, flavorings, relishes, Worcestershire sauce, stock food and paints.

One by one, the items were shown the Senators and he told them each came out of the peanut.

"He has made the most wonderful exhibit ever presented to the Committee," said John Nance Garner, later Vice-President of the United States. Needless to tell, the bill passed.

Later a St. Louis paper remarked that Carver showed the Committee that a hundred and forty-five products could be made out of the peanut.

"We are just beginning to find out what the peanut is and the part it can be made to play in the role of human economy," he said shortly afterwards at his Tuskegee laboratory to a group of friends. "Here is a bottle of peanut cream. It can be used in coffee, chocolate, cereal fruits and in other ways, the same as cow's products. Here is peanut milk . . . Not long since I gave it to a neighbor and invited myself over to eat it . . . I am honest when I say that it was the finest I had ever tasted. Here is a bottle of peanut coffee, instant coffee. Because of its superior food value the peanut should become almost a universal diet for man."

It was this Senate appearance which threw the scientist into the national limelight. He was declared at the time to have "out-Burbanked Burbank with his peanut discoveries," and was called "the peanut wizard." He had done the same thing for other products, but it was his peanut discoveries which touched the match to popular fancy. Dr. Monroe Work said to the author recently that when he first heard Dr. Carver in 1904 at a Georgia conference, he was presented as the "sweet potato wizard." However the peanut was destined to be his popularizing agent.

He attracted great attention at conferences, fairs and exhibitions when he displayed a pint of peanut milk, which he said was "rich, creamy and palatable." While working with the peanut, he discovered that he could make milk on which cream would rise, that could be churned into butter.

In an article in 1923, the Montgomery (Alabama) *Advertiser* said, "Twenty-five years ago the peanut was 'a no-account,' but today 53,000,000 bushels are produced, with 7,000,000 pounds of peanut butter, and 3,000,000 pounds of oil. All of this came from Carver. His peanut milk, both sweet and sour, can be used in the same ways as cow's milk. The curds can be made into many fancy types of cheese and fillings for pastries."

Two years later the story was released that he had fabricated thirty-two kinds of milk from the peanut.

"I have refused to leave Tuskegee Institute to take up one of the several flattering offers made me by corporations, simply because I believe that it is God's wish that I should develop the commercial possibilities of Southern agricultural products. I believe if I should leave the institute where so much of my work has been a success, my gift would fail me."

During those years very tempting offers to leave Tuskegee were pouring in, one of which came from Thomas Edison, carrying with it a stipend of what has been said to be $175,000. Others offered him from $50,000 to a $100,000 a year, including the "finest laboratory on earth."

To all he turned a deaf ear, for he had devoted his talents to the South, where "I can do the greatest amount of good to the greatest number of my own people." This was an entrancing vision which time did not dim.

"There is no work more important than that you are doing," said Theodore Roosevelt, during the years when Carver was giving the South the peanut industry. Out of all this work, the creation of the peanut industry with its multiplied by-products, the scientist never received so much as a dime. His talents were free to all the people. When offered money for his work, or for any tangible service, he would say, "Mr. Creator did not charge anything to grow the peanut, and I cannot accept money for my work with it."

It was this humble reliance upon divine aid which

made him the great man of science that he was. In him was no boast of human ability, merely the assumption that Mr. Creator, as he familiarly spoke of God, opened doors through which he stepped with his scientific apparatus and together they worked out the products for which he is famed.

"Too many writers and speakers make it appear," said Dr. A. W. Curtis, the scientist whom Dr. Carver selected to carry on his work and to head the Carver Foundation, "that he merely went into his laboratory with a prayer that some new product would jump from the end of his magical stick. This was not the case at all. While he believed in prayer, relied upon divine guidance, he furnished God with the best scientific method and approach possible, and out of this consecrated ability under God's guidance all the results of his life came."

"In other words," I broke in, sitting at Dr. Carver's desk in the Carver Museum as I talked with the brilliant young scientist, "by linking his ability to God's power, he gave the world the hundreds of products which he fabricated from the peanut, sweet potato, clays, pecan and the like." To which the scientist nodded assent, saying, "That is the secret of his success. He was a matchless scientist, supreme in his field, who asked God to use his techniques and training to the best advantage."

God Draws the Curtain Aside . . .

"Without God to draw aside the curtain, I would be helpless . . .

"No books ever go into my laboratory. The thing that I am to do and the way of doing it come to me. I never grope for methods, the method is revealed at the moment I am inspired to create something new . . .

"I never received any money from my discoveries. The other day someone sent me a hundred dollars, but I sent it back to him. God does not charge for His work, neither can I in working with Him."

—From an address delivered in New York City, 1923

CHAPTER VI

THE FRUITS OF FAME

George Washington Carver had climbed at last to the hill's crest, and at sixty was recognized as a famed scientist, whose reliance was upon God and whose methods were orderly, yet revealed. It had been a long trek from those boyhood days spent in the woods of the plantation in search of truth. Many had been the difficulties which threatened to crowd him from the achiever's path. He never asked the price any discovery demanded, merely paid it humbly and persevered in the tasks of his laboratory until in the end he had succeeded.

"Three hundred products from the peanut alone," men said glibly in accounting his results, as though each leaped from the crucible of experimentation with the flip of a mental thumb. Not so. Behind every discovery were years of investigation and experimentation in his laboratory. Since those long-away farm days, four o'clock each morning, summer and winter, was his getting-up time. Out in the woods by dawn, talking with the Creator, communing with Nature's visible forms, listening to the varied language she speaks, and then back into the laboratory, where the results of the morning were brewed into workable forms — this was his life.

On the surface it appeared that everything came easily, with little effort and no drudgery. But the hours he spent in the laboratory testify to the orderliness of his scientific approach to any problem, and, like an Edison or a Pasteur, each discovery cost him the scientist's price. He fought his way up from Simpson College, through a complete training at the Iowa State College, and during the years Booker T. was clamoring for more poultry production, the scientist in him drove Carver unrelentingly to the laboratory to test every seed, each remedy, all products.

On the hundreds of Tuskegee's seed plots, he faithfully worked to produce better farm results that the South's farmers might thereby benefit. Those years of practical application of the scientific method to the farmers' and the housewives' problems were strenuous ones. While the labors of those years produced little immediate recognition, they laid the foundation for his lasting fame. From Carver's earliest days at the Institute his investigations proceeded along three tangible lines of research, each of which was sufficient to cause him to be an enrollee in any Hall of Fame.

1. First in importance, though not in his estimation, were the commercial products to be made from peanuts, pecans, sweet potatoes, clays and herbs. It was this line of investigation which shot him into the limelight of public acclaim. But this was not in his scheme the most important. The second field in which he 2. gained success was that of teaching. Even Booker T. Washington during the time when he was declaring, "You are no farmer . . . you cannot raise chickens . . . you know nothing about ducks," was rightly saying, "As a teacher few men have the ability to inspire and train as you."

From the first year at Tuskegee, he carried a heavy teaching schedule, averaging during those earlier years from eighteen to twenty teaching hours a week.

He taught such courses as Beginning Agriculture, Senior Agriculture, Cattle Raising, Poultry, Farm Management, and often in his introductory classes he covered the entire range of agricultural subjects.

Carver at first was reluctant to tear himself away from the laboratory where grand plans were brewing for farm aid and commercial improvements, and he told the president that he was through with teaching. The students, however, had other ideas on the subject.

"And when Carver said he would teach no other classes, it was not Booker T.," said friend Williston in bringing out of the past many topics on which the writers had been vague, "but it was the students that demanded he teach them. From the student appeal he could not turn away. They came to him the very first fall term when his laboratory had been established, and asked him to teach them. The result was he always taught a few classes until during his last dozen or so years."

The lure of shaping student personality was always supreme to the scientist. He was a peanut wizard true enough, but in the handling of youth, the carving of character, he felt just as much at home as in the field of scientific research. Many are the stories which students tell concerning his interest in them. Too busy for famous visitors who often came to see him for curiosity's sake, as one would go to view Grant's Tomb, the Lincoln Memorial or the Grand Canyon, he nevertheless always had time for young people who came to his laboratory.

"If an athlete would sprain a limb, he would take his bottle of peanut oil and spend hours working on the lad until he had gained the use of the leg again," said a Tuskegee friend. "There are a dozen white boys here in the city of Tuskegee that he took his time to treat."

It was the call of youth that sent him out of his way to inspire and train them. Had Carver done nothing else than teach his courses at the Institute, he would have been famous.

3. His popularity rested upon a third line of investigation which was geared to producing workable results for the farmer and no less the housewife. From his first days at the Institute, he demanded of himself improved methods of farming as well as better ways to care for and use the farm's edible products. So important were his achievements in this field that had he done nothing else, the South could never repay the debt owed him.

During the years when Dr. Washington was alive, the scientist kept a constant stream of bulletins flowing into the president's office.

On arriving at Tuskegee, Booker T. told the new professor that he wanted him to work for the Negro's uplift. Dr. Carver often told a story he heard Booker relate of a ship lost at sea, which, on being found by another vessel, ran a signal on its mast, "Water . . . we die of thirst."

The second ship signaled, "Cast down your bucket where you are." The captain followed the injunction, and on bringing up the bucket he found it filled with fresh water, for they were in the mouth of the Amazon River.

During the early years at Tuskegee, Dr. Washington insisted that Carver "cast down his investigating bucket where he was" — in Macon County, Alabama. By doing this Carver found enough in his own vicinity to keep him busy throughout a long and active lifetime. Dr. Carver, in commenting on the speech in which he told the story, said to the president, "I believe this is the solution of the Negro problem." At once he went to work on Macon County and the South's products. As a result of this investigation he produced a series of bulletins — beginning with the first, published in 1898, on "Feeding Acorns" and ending with "Nature's Garden for Victory and Peace," dated October, 1942 — totaling forty-three in all.

These deal with the practical results of his own investigations of the farmer's possibilities in Alabama and surrounding sections. Several have been of local interest only, such as "Some Ornamental Plants of Macon County, Alabama," Bulletin 16, issued in 1909, while others have attracted national attention and aroused world-wide interest.

"Bulletin 43 has not been alone enthusiastically received here in our country," he said in the revised edition of "Nature's Garden for Victory and Peace," "but the British Food Ministry has passed out the following list of wild vegetables selected from Bulletin 43, and urged their use, saying in part 'The following are easily obtainable along rustic lanes and in fields of grass and clover where hitherto they have been a hindrance.

" 'Leading the list are nettles and dandelions, purslane, and that curse of crops, wild mustard. Nettles with the sting cooked out of them are much more palatable eating than spinach; dandelions, whether as a side dish to the roast, made into tea or into wine, are not only medicinal, but good eating and drinking.' "

Carver was eager that the bulletins be more than theory and he insisted upon their being thoroughly practical. For instance, in Bulletin 43 he affirms, "February 27, 1942, found us feasting on the following, as an uncooked salad: Wild lettuce, both *L. sativa* and *L. scorale*, Wild onion, *Antenaria plantagenifolia*, Young oxalis leaves, *Geranium maculatum* and *Stellaria media*. Served with mayonnaise and French dressing."

It was this actual testing of results which sold the farmers upon Carver's work. They came to know that when he produced a bulletin, wrote a farm article, gave a wild vegetable menu, or told them how to pickle and cure meat or advised their wives on the use of peanuts as a table delicacy or a three-times-a-day food, all of it had come out of the crucible of his own living. He was no theorist, but the same scientific acumen which marked his laboratory work went into the production of these bulletins.

Hence each one met a definite need. They were not for the scientific agriculturist or farm chemist, ensconced in the lecturer's chair at a school of agriculture, but were guideposts in the daily routine of the farmer — many of whom had to have the bulletins read to them because of illiteracy among the Negro and white housewife. This is where Carver "cast down his bucket," and on bringing it up was careful that the "living waters" would satisfy a current requirement.

Each bulletin, as he finished the experimentation and wrote his findings, indicated a then-vital need which he was trying to satisfy. As they appeared year by year they also pointed out the scientist's growing interests. They likewise covered the entire range of agricultural and home economic activities in which farm folk engaged.

In broad divisions they represented distinct phases of the farmer's problems, such as: (1) soil building; (2) cotton growing; (3) sweet potato raising; (4) growth of cow-peas; (5) corn raising; (6) wild plum conservation; (7) gardening for the farmer; (8) dairying and dairy products; (10) raising small grain crops; (11) poultry raising; (12) pickling and cure of meat; (13) home canning of fruits and vegetables; (14) fertilizers for the farm; (15) home menus; (16) hog and cattle raising; (17) orchards on the farm; (18) alfalfa raising; (19) growing and canning tomatoes; (20) the peanut and how to use it; (21) use of native clays.

More than half the bulletins were produced during his first fifteen years at the Institute. His first, published in 1898 at the instigation of Dr. Washington, was a simple bulletin dealing with the problem of feeding acorns to farm animals, especially pigs.

Immediately he began experimenting with the sweet potato, since it was the key to unlock the greatest blessings for the farmer. In 1898 he published Bulletin No. 2, "Experiments with Sweet Potatoes." By 1906 Bulletin No. 10 was issued on a similar subject, "Saving the Sweet Potato Crop." Bulletin No. 17, 1910, was "Possibilities of the Sweet Potato in Macon County, Alabama." In an enlarged form and revised throughout this was issued as No. 30 in 1915, when the World War I years called for the conservation of foodstuffs. No. 37, "How to Make Sweet Potato Flour, Starch, Bread, Sugar and Mock Cocoanut," appeared in 1918 and was his contribution to our war effort. No. 38, issued the same year and entitled, "How the Farmer Can Save His Sweet Potatoes," carried the message of crop and food conservation further than his previous bulletin.

His purpose here was to show the farmer, no less the government, the value of the sweet potato for human consumption as well as for stock feed. In Bulletin No. 38 he gives thirty-two practical methods for using the sweet potato as food, including sweet potato pie, stuffed sweet potatoes, croquettes, balls, puree, baked with apples, muffins, doughnuts, savories and sweet potato nuts. In the same bulletin he gives his method for making sweet potato flour, the basis of which is to slice the potato thin, dry it in the sun or in a drier, and then grind it as fine as possible. The final step is bolting this through a cloth "in the same way as for other flours."

In each of his handling methods he was as thorough as he was with the sweet potato. The cow-pea was always for him an amazing article of food, and Bulletin 5, published in 1903, is the first of a series on the food. In 1908 this was followed by No. 13, "How to Cook Cow-Peas," to be trailed in 1911 by No. 19, entitled, "Some Possibilities of the Cow-Pea in Macon County." The wild plum held an interest for him in that it was plentiful in his part of Alabama and his first bulletin on the subject, No. 12, was entitled, "Saving the Wild Plum," which was matched ten years later in 1917 with "Forty-three Ways to Save the Wild Plum Crop."

In his "Pickling and Curing of Meat," No. 24, issued in 1912, he not only outlined curing methods which can be used in hot weather but gave an ingeniously worked out series of menus using this cured meat. In all there are forty-four such methods listed, outlining four specific plans by which pig's feet are made edible. With Dr. Carver, even to the end, pig's feet were a delicacy which graced his finest and most select meals.

James Lomax, who for the last four years of Carver's life was the scientist's private dietician, blessed by the doctor with the simpler title of "my boy," relates how in his declining years the great man insisted upon having pig's feet regularly.

"I went into the kitchen," said the hostess of Dorthy Hall, "and opened the refrigerator to find a large pan filled with pig's feet. When I asked the cook who they were for, she said, 'Dr. Carver.' 'Why, he's a sick man,' I said. The cook answered, 'He declares pig's feet are what keeps his blood in good shape and him alive. It's the gelatin in them, he says.' " The doctor's love for this delicacy moved him, in giving his first method of boiling them, to make the notation "Extra Fine" in his Bulletin No. 24.

By studying these bulletins one can trace the scientist's interests from year to year. On first arriving at Tuskegee one of his major problems was that of soil conditioning by means of proper fertilizers; so in Bulletin No. 3, 1899, he published "Fertilizer Experiment with Cotton." Solving the fertilizer problem to his own satisfaction, he omitted this from his leaflets and bulletins until 1916 when the World War shut off the supply of commercial fertilizers, and he crystallized his thought on substitute fertilizers and those close at the farmer's hand in a leaflet called, "What Shall We Do For Fertilizer This Year?"

One of his prime interests was cotton, which has always been the South's most dependable crop, and on arriving at the Institute he began to make a specific study of it. The third bulletin discussed this topic in connection with the use of fertilizer to increase the output. Bulletin No. 6 was printed in 1906, entitled, "Cotton Growing on Sandy Upland Soils," to be followed two years later by No. 14, "How To Make Cotton Growing Pay"; the next publication, a leaflet, appeared in 1915 and was entitled, "A New and Prolific Variety of Cotton." He was loyal to King Cotton till the last of his days, and one of his final experiments had to do with the successful use of cotton in road building, many tests of which were made under his supervision. He proved to himself that cotton used properly in asphalts and concretes would improve the quality of paved roads.

Carver loved the tomato, for it was a veritable source of vitamins and could be used to form any number of combinations for menus. In 1918, when the ravages of the war shut off many usable foodstuffs, he published Bulletin No. 36, entitled, "How to Grow the Tomato and 115 Ways to Prepare it for the Table." His discussion of the subject was as thorough as usual, but the menus and uses for the tomato are supreme among all the foods he prepared for the table.

Here are some of the recipes he gives: Green tomato jam, made by cooking green tomatoes, loaf sugar and preserved ginger; tomatoes stuffed with corn; tomato omelet, cooking the tomato with scrambled or whipped eggs; tomato marmalade, using lemons and raisins; tomato butter and jam; tomato souffle; tomato stuffed with shrimp, baked with eggs — "Scoop out . . . to hold broken egg. Do not break the yolk, season and bake in moderate oven until tomato is tender. Serve on rounds of buttered toast with cream sauce." In 115 different ways he shows the farmer how to make use of the tomato on his table, and each method was tested by the scientist before it was written for the bulletin.

There is literally no end to the amazing list of practical experiments Carver carried on to benefit the Southland farmer, whether white or colored. He taught the women how to can and preserve fruits and vegetables in a bulletin entitled, "When, What and How to Can and Preserve Fruits and Vegetables in the Home." He showed the farmer how to smudge his orchards with "native materials in Alabama."

In each of the forty-three bulletins produced he was practical in his advice and whether teaching the farmer how to grow pigs, his wife how to "meet the new economic conditions in the South," or the school children "how to grow vegetables," he had tested each item he used in his bulletins. Multiplied thousands of Southlanders learned from him the various methods by which they could produce their own foodstuffs, vary their diet by a table garden, and at the same time get away from a pork-and-meal-three-times-a-day existence.

He had come up the hard-scrabble way. When he was a child on the plantation, he faced near-starvation after the ravages of the Civil War had wrecked the Carver plantation. When he worked his way through school, whether living on a suet-and-meal diet or faring slightly better with the addition of an occasional pork chop, he was never far away from the insistent demands of hunger.

In the interim between high school graduation and college days, he tried his hand at being a true

Westerner, and settled on a homestead two miles south of the small town of Beeler, Kansas. Building his own sod hut, he put in what crops he thought would be successful, only to discover that if he was to keep from starving to death he would have to take a ranch job with the Gregg-Steeley Livestock Ranch. Grand as those days were, still he was as constantly close to hunger as at any period in his life. Hence when Tuskegee's call was answered, the remembrance of his own problems of finding enough food to live on whetted his desire to provide a practical solution for the Southern farmers.

An interesting side light on those homestead days is revealed by Frank Beeler, writing years later in the Highland *Vidette*. "My mother and other ladies took an interest in this good orphan Christian boy," says Mr. Beeler. After he secured a job on the Gregg-Steeley ranch "he carried on his music, painting and studies. Mr. Steeley was a fine violinist, Mr. Gregg, a good guitarist, George was an organist and I played the B flat cornet. I look back with a great deal of satisfaction to the concerts we pulled off in the sod houses and also in my store . . . Those were days of real joy. Realizing that agriculture was a dismal failure in this dry country, really fit for grazing only, friend George sold out and left for Iowa."

It was this realization which haunted "friend George" throughout his career and he could not be content until "I did something about it."

During those early years, as Beeler says, the spiritual interest of his life ran high — which continued to be a dominant characteristic of his life.

When the South faced economic ruin because of the boll weevil's ravages as it swept from Mexico into

Texas and thence across man-made border lines until each Southern state was held captive by it, Dr. Carver focused his attention upon this problem with a scientific definiteness until he had found the solution. King Cotton had been the South's cash crop, and now that it was gravely threatened, something must be found to take its place.

George looked upon this as his own dilemma, and took the issue with him into the laboratory. Long in the early morning hours he sought the unlocking key to the mystery. He knew the Creator had something which could take cotton's place. There were other crops available which he checked one by one. Cowpeas lacked sufficient varied possibilities to be the "answer to the Southern farmer's prayer."

Looking long at the records he had made concerning sweet potato production and the different uses to which it could be put, he almost decided this was to be cotton's competitor. Taking it into the laboratory, he tore the sweet potato apart, discovered of what it consisted, and then by the slow process of synthesis began putting those chemical elements together in different combinations. What had been the yellow yam of the Southern table was transformed into a very usable starch. It turned into sugars, leaped the boundaries of its constituent elements, became a very delicious bread, and could be used also in loaves, muffins and biscuits.

Patiently Carver continued his investigation, coddling the potato, and carving its secrets from its until-then-locked treasure house, until out leaped more than 118 different things which he made from it. However of them all, only one seemed destined to be a cash product. The sweet potato still remained primarily a table dish, and though it played a part in many products devised by the wizard of the laboratory, its favorite role was as a food.

For awhile it did look as if the sweet potato, "our most prolific crop," as he expressed it, would turn into a cash enterprise for the South when a starch manufacturing company sprang up in Laurel, Mississippi, and from the 1936 sweet potato produced a half-million pounds of starch.

Carver next went to the pecan, and searched through its possibilities, only to discover that of the seventy to ninety products he was able to fabricate from its amazing potentialities, none of them could be sufficiently dramatized to take cotton's place as a cash rewarder of the farmer's labors. He tried clays and though out of this rich source of usable products he was able to make numerous dyes, paint stains and the richest of colors, as old as the hills and as permanent as the blue of the sky, still clay was not the answer.

There was, however, another product to investigate. He had been dabbling with its capabilities, but each time, for years, had come away from his crucibles disappointed. The peanut, as the editor expressed it, was a "no-account." It was too hard to bring to peanut-manhood and as an edible it was more satisfactory for hogs than humans.

Following his usual routine of work for each day, he began to discuss the peanut with his Creator. "I get up every morning, winter and summer at four," he said on Lincoln's Birthday, 1934, speaking to his friends at the Institute. "First I go into the woods and gather specimens, and listen to what God has to say to me. After I have had my morning talk with

God, I go to my laboratory and begin to carry out His wishes for the day, and if I fail it's my failure, and if I succeed then God's will has been done."

One morning, following this plan, he came back to the laboratory in search for the unique solution to the immediate problem of successfully defending the South's economic life against the boll weevil's devastation, and began to talk with the Creator.

"Years ago, I went into my laboratory and said, 'Dear Creator, please tell me what the universe was made for.' " Often he told this story in his famous lectures given before university student bodies and popular conclaves throughout the South.

"Said the Creator, 'You want to know too much for such a little mind as yours. Ask for something your size.'

"Then I asked, 'Dear Creator, tell me what man was made for.' Again the great Creator replied, 'Little one, you are still asking too much. Bring down the extent of your request.'

" 'Tell me then, Creator, what the peanut was made for.'

"Then the great Creator taught me how to take the peanut apart and put it together again. And out of this came all these products which the Creator taught me to make."

"The greatest of all the kingdoms, the animal, the vegetable and the mineral, is the fourth which the Creator has added, the synthetic kingdom," said Dr. Carver in his later days.

Exploring this synthetic kingdom of the peanut, the master scientist found an entirely new field of commerce for the South. Out of that simple little talk, repeated many times over, has come a yearly business amounting to a quarter of a billion dollars. It has put cash in the pockets of the Southern farmer — pockets which after the cotton crash just before the first World War were empty. "The no-account peanut" now rides on the crest of a high financial wave. Little did Carver dream that he would see the time when peanut butter would sell for forty cents a pound, and when the humble oil of the ground nut, as he often spoke of it, would cost nearly a dollar a pint.

His ingenuity, directed by divine guidance, created a "big business" enriching thousands, yet from it he never received a single dollar for his services, nor did he wish for one. When asked why he returned checks sent gratuitously to him in return for some scientific service to peanut growers and processors, his characteristic remark was, "The Creator did not charge to grow the peanut, no more can I charge for my services."

He looked upon his research with the peanut as a divine task to which he had been appointed, and his ability to delve into the peanut and discover its untold sources of products to him was a stewardship entrusted by the Almighty. Little wonder then that he could say, "There is nothing I can explain. I reach out my hand and there it is. The thing I am about to do always comes to me. I do not have to grope. I have never had to. The method has always been revealed to me. There comes suddenly the inspiration to create something. I reach out my hand and there it is. The thing is done. And it is right."

When he discovered the royal blue with which the tombs of the Egyptian kings were painted, a paint which is indestructible and does not fade though centuries have passed, his happy remark was, "God made the clay in the hills. He made it in Egypt . . . Why should it not be permanent? It has been there for centuries — unchanged. All I do is to compound what God made for man's use and delight."

The coloration of this royal blue has been declared by scientists, artists and paint manufacturers to be unsurpassed, and seventy times bluer than the bluest paint yet fabricated. Carver's answer was terse when asked how he did it. To him there was no miracle. God who had painted the clays in the Alabama hills and ravines with the elements had made them unfading, and when the divine Hand guided the consecrated scientist to them and revealed the process by which they should be separated from the other colors, he said, "No miracle, simply a revelation of the proper method to use."

After he had unlocked the secrets of the peanut, his activities in the laboratory were so intense that it was almost impossible to keep a proper tabulation of the number of products he was able to make from the lowly ground nut. In 1923, speaking to a group during one of his exhibitions, he said, "I have made thirty-two different kinds of milk from the peanut." During the same year his record showed some three hundred products from clay, more than a hundred from the sweet potato, and one hundred and sixteen from the peanut. Before walking out of his laboratory for the last time, Carver had pushed to three hundred the number of products which he had been able to dig from the hidden depths of the peanut.

When, in 1925, the Florida orange growers sought his assistance in opening new markets for their crops, he combined a peanut milk with orange juice, causing it to have the appearance and the food qualities of cow's milk while possessing also the delicate flavoring of the orange. The same year saw his name in *Who's Who* with the list of his accomplishments.

"America knows no more inspiring story than that of Carver," said the *Success* Magazine, August 22, 1925, "the homeless Negro boy who won his way to an education through the barrier of poverty and race feelings and became one of America's foremost scientists. Dr. Carver's life has been consecrated to the service of Christ and science, which he knows are inseparable."

One of the fruits of growing fame was the high privilege of speaking extensively to colleges throughout the South and East. During January, 1925, Carver spoke at the University of North Carolina under the auspices of the Y.M.C.A. At this meeting, as was his custom while speaking to college students, he opened his heart to them, telling them the technique of his discoveries.

"I always sleep over a problem," he said on January 21 to the students in revealing how he had made the yolk of an egg from the sweet potato. "I never open my mail until after supper . . . I go to sleep with them [problems] on my mind, and the next morning I see the method and the new perspective which usually clears it up. I didn't do it. God has only used me to reveal some of His wonderful providences."

From this time on George Washington Carver's name was known throughout his nation. His was a rightly won fame. He had achieved by producing results not for himself but for the people with whom he lived and from whom he sprang. From that moment till his work was finished he was an inspiration to America's Negro youth. While visiting the Carver Museum for the first time, a young colored soldier was looking at the marvelous samples of paints and stains, which the doctor had displayed on boards hanging from the wall. The youth discovered the purpose of my Tuskegee visit, introduced himself and said:

"Negro youth look to Dr. Carver's life work with its world prominence, his mastery of agricultural chemistry, his magnificent achievements, and his devout, religious manifestations as being one not only of a scientist but as another martyr worthy of emulation. As Abraham Lincoln brought new hope to the people of America in the dark pre-Civil War days, so do the achievements of Dr. Carver mean a new hope to Negro youth."

Private Emanuel B. Walker, Jr., expresses the sentiment which stirs in the heart of colored youth everywhere. "He thought not of tributes," said the soldier, "when he produced a new product, but exclaimed that if the good Lord bestowed within him the genius of creative power, then the results did not belong to him, but to the people who work in the fields, factories, mines — to all humanity."

THE TRAIL BLAZER'S VIEWPOINTS . . .

"When you can do the common things of life in an uncommon way, you will command the attention of the world . . .

"Creative genius is what makes people respect you. It isn't a color question, it's a question of whether you have what the world wants . . .

"You never saw a heavy thinker with his mouth open. Stop talking so much . . .

"A personal relationship with the great Creator of all things is the only foundation for the abundant life. Walk and talk with God and let Him direct your path. Some people never really touch life because they are bound up in themselves . . . You must get in touch with the Creator if you want to be lifted above the little things of life."

—From various Carver addresses

Chapter VII

EMISSARY OF GOODWILL

"What I am creating is not in any book," said Dr. Carver in an address at Akron, Ohio, April 12, 1925. "I have become a book maker. When I get an inspiration I go into the laboratory and God tells me what to do. What I have done with the sweet potato and the peanut can be done with all the things of earth. God has said that every herb and plant that He has created can be made of use to mankind, if we will only put our hand in His and let Him help us.

"There are over three hundred things that can be made from Alabama clay — things that will rival the old Egyptian art work in blues, greens, mauves and brown. God is going to reveal to us the things He has never revealed before, if we will only put our hand in His for guidance."

During the last eighteen years of his life, this was the Carver message which he proclaimed on the lecture platform, in written articles, and in newspapers. The teacher had written the story of his personality upon the character of his students, and within a few years more he was to step from the classroom forum to the larger lecture platform of the nation. The bulk of his finest experiments had already been finished. He had delved into the peanut's secrets until it was almost possible for mankind to live by it alone. The sweet potato, the pecan, Alabama clays, wild vegetables as edibles had told him their story, and in his files he had pigeonholed the formulas by which this magic could be made useful to his fellow man.

The massive research of his life was done, but there remained the finer task of carrying this message to the people. Hence the last two decades of his life were largely devoted to the task of being an emissary of goodwill to the nation. His people had often been misunderstood. The race which nursed him, colored his skin to a dark ebony, had long been an under-privileged people, and it was the scientist's work to create a better understanding of them and to show that the color of a man's skin made no difference in the accomplishment of a life devoted to scientific research and to God.

"A group of white men here"—said Carver, speaking at Tulsa, Oklahoma, where he had been summoned by oil men to discover additional oil possibilities — "say they want a man who can locate oil more accurately. They forgot to say whether they wanted a white man, a red man, a yellow or a black man; they only said they wanted a man who could locate oil."

This was the supreme test of a man's worth to the community, irrespective of the color of his skin. Resident within the individual, Carver felt, the Creator had placed certain abilities, which if consecrated to a human service and God-directed would lift the sky-line of possibilities for the race. Coloration made no difference in this ability, if properly developed and handled.

The South looked upon the scientist's work as that of trail blazing. He did not turn his researches into cash, but rather pointed out the potentialities of what lay within the South's reach.

"His answer to the suggested commercialization of his products is: 'I am a trail blazer,'" said Wade

Moss of the Tom Houston Peanut Company, Columbus, Georgia, writing in 1930. "He has shown the South wherein its wealth lies. Much like the prospector, he has sought the mine, and then left it to others to obtain the gold. The South does not expect Dr. Carver to develop his vast researches; to do this would take ten lifetimes of one man . . . "

Moss was director of a business to which the scientist's research had given birth, years earlier, and recently the same concern refused an offer of more than two million dollars if they would sell out. There were also many businesses, based upon the ebony wizard's researches, which were within the reach of financial genius and awaited only development.

Going into Macon County's mud banks, he came out with shovelfuls of red clays, which through six successive processes of oxidation became the lost royal blue of the Egyptian tombs, and has been described as "seventy times bluer than the bluest blue." If oxidized a few more times it becomes royal purple.

"Here is an opportunity for some Southern industry to go on with the work," said Dr. Carver, "to build the necessary laboratory, find out the properties of the soil of Macon County, or any of the other Southern counties, and then learn to make this pigment or whatever pigments are required by the paint manufacturer."

Look into any year during these last two decades of his life, and you will find the scientist standing on some lecture platform declaring this message of interracial goodwill and freely offering commercial possibilities within the reach of whatever hands will delve into nature's secrets and link them to usable forms.

He took time, however, to carry on experiments as his genius indicated or the divine will, according to his terminology, led him.

"One Sunday I heard a minister tell of a missionary with tuberculosis who had to return home to die," he said on April 12, 1925, as an instance of his humanitarian inclinations. "I did not hear any of his sermon, but I kept hearing a Voice say, 'Can't you find something that will help other missionaries and other people so that they will not have to die of this disease?' I went straight to my laboratory after church and from some peanuts I made a creosote emulsion that has proven very good for pulmonary troubles. I have taken the emulsion and cured myself of a cough . . . Peanuts are a food and a medicine combined."

Let us observe his activities on the lecture platform during several years. On January 25, 1925, for instance, he spoke at the North Carolina College for Women, where he displayed his products of interest to the housewife. December 18 of the following year, we find him at Knoxville, Tennessee, discussing his researches before the Teachers' Association of the State. On May 7, he was declaring the usableness of his products at Doddsville, Mississippi, where his address was under the auspices of the city schools. On New Year's Day, 1927, he went to Kingstone, North Carolina, where he spoke and demonstrated his products, including a new rubber substitute, of which he said, "It looks good to me."

By September 2 of that year he was at the Tennessee State Fair, where he exhibited his discoveries during the past thirty years, including oleomargarine, chili sauce, and dozens of other foods. During 1928 he toured twenty-eight Virginia and Tennessee colleges, speaking under the sponsorship of the Y.M.C.A. Interracial Committee. These addresses were given before the largest and most important college student bodies in the states, and at each place he was well received. Receptive audiences lingered long after the formal lectures were finished and bombarded him with a barrage of questions.

During the year he was a speaker before the American Association for the Advancement of Science, held at Columbia University. From here he jumped to Fort Worth, Texas, appearing at the State Fair, and he finished the year's jaunts by a trip to Tampa, Florida, where he "found many uses for the palmetto root, discovering it to be rich in sodium, potassium and other alkaloidal properties, and also located in the green persimmon a rich source of dyes."

Until now no college had thought of honoring him with the degree of Doctor, but he had so pushed himself into the national limelight that his alma mater, Simpson College, granted him the title Doctor of Science. Of all the men who have been graced with this distinction, few have ever carried it with greater worth than the colored lad, now grown to manhood, who was traded for a race horse.

The following year, 1929, on November 10, he announced that he had succeeded in making marble from sawdust, and today one may sit on the marble bench which was fabricated in his laboratory from common sawdust, clay and a liberal amount of his own wizardry. For this achievement he was acclaimed by newspaper editorials throughout the nation. Had any genius arisen to further develop this suggested plan a new industry would have sprung up in the South.

Shortly after this he spoke to the Columbus, Georgia, Lions Club, being presented by a state senator, at which time he made a public display of paper and beaverboard that he concocted from peanut hulls. He could not forget the peanut, even though he had passed by most of his important discoveries and always, even to his last months, he kept working at peanut brews and experimentations. During the last year of his life, he announced through Dr. Curtis, his assistant, that peanut hulls could be successfully used in soils for lightening loams, preparing for proper drainage, and similar purposes — hitherto accomplished only by the strength of years-old peat moss.

Pictures of the doctor which were taken at this time show him wearing a bat-wing collar, neat handmade tie, lapel flower and a properly trimmed mustache. His clothes had not yet attained that look of having been "cut by a Southern ax" and vintaged in the pre-Civil War days — an appearance they would later assume.

"I could not talk when I was nineteen," he said on May 9, 1931, speaking at Christiansburg, Virginia, when a touch of usual humor showed through the seriousness of his address. "Now when I tell people that, sometimes they say, 'What a pity he ever learned to talk.' Young people, I came near saying fellow students, I want to advise you to get in touch with real things — with nature and the things around you . . . I rode all the way from Atlanta up here, and had a chance to see nature . . .

"I saw a person the other day who told me that he

had the blues. I wondered why he didn't have the pinks, reds, yellows. They are all beautiful and lovely. Yet he had the blues only and was disgruntled with nature and did not enjoy nature at all . . .

"Friends, always learn this lesson: think before you act. Don't do things rashly and then have to regret it . . . Ninety-nine per cent of the failures come from people who have the habit of making excuses."

In October of that year he experimented with the use of cotton in making paving blocks, and made three squares which consisted of seventy-five per cent low-grade cotton. The paving was smooth, firm, and not in the least crumbly. Later he was to see the same paving tested in Mississippi and other states for permanent use in road-making. It was on October 21 that he announced for the first time the fact that he had succeeded in churning the cream from his peanut milk.

"George W. Carver is a man that truly overcometh," said Robert Barry of the Tom Houston Peanut Company, in presenting him with a bas-relief of himself, in honor of his achievements with the peanut. "Men have made rules of success . . . but the one source of all unchanging knowledge is the Bible . . . George W. Carver has learned to co-ordinate the three God-given agents, soul, mind and body. It is with great pleasure that I witness the unveiling of this bas-relief, this likeness in bronze of one so great as he."

On the occasion the Birmingham *News* said, "Dr. Carver is one of Alabama's most distinguished citizens. The people of this state may be proud of him, and glad of the honor that was paid him last Thursday" — the occasion of the unveiling at Tuskegee Institute.

'Thirty-one was an active year for the traveling scientist. Often he packed his case of products, boarded train or bus, and was bundled off to some college where he spoke on such themes as: "Every herb that beareth seed to you it shall be for meat," or "The earth is full of riches." Touring Southern colleges, he reached a new high in popularity, and wherever he went the largest auditoriums were packed with students eager to hear him.

"Our young people today are smart and not all of youth is frivolous," he said at an Atlanta college. "I am interested to note that there are more creative minds in youth today than of old." On this occasion he told of his success in making new and unusual products from rock and building stone of his county.

During 1931, Josef Stalin, then deep in building his Five-Year Plan, sent an invitation for Dr. Carver to visit the Soviet Union that he might aid the cotton industry. Said the Russian representative, "If it meets with your approval I shall also arrange a tour for you through the Soviet Union to demonstrate your findings in the field of agriculture."

While the doctor declined the offer, he did arrange for a substitute to make the journey. "I am grateful to learn of your proposition," he said. "Now as to going myself I am not sure whether my strength will permit it . . . It may be necessary to find a younger person, which can be done."

His interests also leaped to another nation, and during this year he devised a vegetarian menu for Gandhi, including a soybean milk, which proved popular with the famous Indian leader. Later he added a peanut milk to the list of edibles which Gandhi found invigorating and refreshing.

The following year saw an intensification of the doctor's lecture tours; he crossed state boundaries with his products and everywhere drew crowds to hear him. His tours took him to Kansas, Iowa, Indiana, Colorado, Illinois, Oklahoma, Chicago and Washington, D. C., as well as to various states bordering Alabama.

"Prepare yourself to do something," he said on February 8, lecturing to the Good Shepherd Congregational Church, Chicago, on which trip he was accompanied by Dr. Monroe Work. "The most pathetic thing I have seen in recent years was a young Negro who wanted to come South and do something, but couldn't because all he had learned was the regular academic work, and to play the piano a little bit."

An odd case faced the doctor during this year, when a young German youth, who had heard his lecture in an Ohio college, hiked to Dayton only to discover he had missed meeting Dr. Carver, and thence he walked to Atlanta, again to repeat the missing process. On arriving at Tuskegee, he asked to enroll as a student in the Institute, only to learn that the color line kept him out — as the same color distinction years earlier had locked the doors of another university to young George — but on meeting and talking with the scientist, he said:

"I am glad I came. Just these few hours with Dr. Carver are worth the trip."

A Washington, D. C. newspaper said on November 14, 1932, "And now he has made two hundred and eighty-five products from the peanut." The reporter affords us a vivid look at the straggling scientist as he goes about the city's streets:

"He wore an ancient golfing cap, a saggy green alpaca coat, and a pair of brown checked, hand-patched trousers, topping this color scheme with a bright green necktie" — likewise hand-fabricated. "However, the saggy coat covered a bachelor of science, master of science, honorary doctor of science, winner of the Spingarn Medal, member of the Royal Society for the Encouragement of Arts and Manufacturing of Britain."

As he spoke from state to state many calls came to him requesting that he help solve local production and processing problems. Until now there was usually time for these requests, but while he was fulfilling a speaking engagement in Wichita, Kansas, the farmers begged him to find some new uses for their wheat, and he was forced to say no.

"I cannot take the time," he told them in turning a deaf ear to their call for assistance. "My work is with Southern products. I must first help the people at home."

Speaking at Oklahoma City, September 27, he reversed mental gears and raced through the goodnesses of God to him since he first began his long trek, saying, "The Lord has been mighty good to this old Negro . . . " At the height of his popularity he saw that it was the hand of God which led him from conquest to victory, and the lectures given at this time bore the deep stamp of his religious attitude. If success crowned his work, the glory went to God, but if failure blighted his efforts, "It is my failure."

Henry Ford, with whom he enjoyed a long and fruitful friendship, sent an invitation to Carver, while the scientist was speaking at the Farmers' Exchange in Tuscaloosa, Alabama, requesting him to visit and consult with his engineers. Many were the times this invitation was repeated during the doctor's life. One of Carver's final long trips was made to Detroit, for during his last spring he visited that city, where he was honored by Ford, who had built for him at the Greenfield Village the George Washington Carver Memorial Cabin.

Every state in the Union contributed boards or logs for the memorial cabin, some of which are: shortleaf pine, from Alabama; ponderosa pine, Arizona; oak, Arkansas; redwood, California; blue spruce, Colorado; yellow oak, Connecticut; holly, District of Columbia; cabbage palm and cypress, Florida; live oak, Georgia; western white pine, Idaho; tulip tree, Indiana; magnolia, Louisiana; American elm, Massachusetts; apple, Michigan; and white pine from Minnesota.

Small logs were brought from each state and cut into the desired boards at the village sawmill. In the living room, Dr. Carver's home state, Missouri, is represented by a mantlepiece of white oak, Other spots in the building held pieces of piñon pine, white ash, hard maple, green ash, buckeye from Ohio, dogwood, mesquite and pecan from Texas. Truly Carver, whose life had blessed every state in the Union, was honored by their gifts from nature's storehouse, from which he so lavishly drew his products.

When Henry Ford came to build his school at Ways, Georgia, he made it a memorial to the Negro scientist, after whom it was named. It has often been reported that the industrialist tried many times to pry the doctor away from Tuskegee, but always the roots of his interest held him firm at the Institute, which had been the scene of his triumphs in the laboratory. However great the financial rewards Ford held before Carver's eyes, they could in no wise equal "the thousand dollars a year for which I have worked all these years, having never asked for nor received a raise in salary," as he wrote Booker T. just before World War I.

Carver's use of peanut oil as a remedy for infantile paralysis threw him strongly to the fore in newspapers and magazines in 1933 when it was announced at Savannah, Georgia, that "the oil might cure President Roosevelt." Dr. Carver, it must be recalled, during his college days had been the football "rubber" or masseur at Ames, and many wonderful miracles had seemingly come from his hands as he worked with the popular athletes. The magic of those fingers, directed by a brain that knew physical anatomy perfectly, could trace the weakened muscles, and with the blended peanut oil as an instrument for healing, excellent results were obtained at the Tuskegee laboratory as he treated the folk who sought his aid for their withered arms and legs.

In a large glassed-in case at the Carver Museum one may now view some of the five thousand or more letters which flooded the doctor's mail — letters carrying the one request, "Will peanut oil heal me? Where can I obtain information about its use? . . . I am an infantile paralysis sufferer . . . " Carefully the doctor answered each inquiry, giving the desired information, adding what he thought would be the right technique for the treatment. His great compassion for the sufferers as they came to the laboratory caused him to reserve Saturday afternoons and Sundays for a long period of time that he might treat those who came to him for assistance.

But few cases did he ever turn away, and not a dollar came to him for any treatment. In some instances he was unable to do any good for those who called. Glenn Clark tells of a man who brought his son to the doctor for treatment, only to be refused. When the man profanely asked why the scientist could not help his son, he answered:

"Because my prayers and the power of this ointment would never be able to penetrate all the profanity in your heart. The profanity is enough to block any healing power from reaching anyone."

In each case the prayers of the believing Negro were combined with the technique of the skilled anatomist as the peanut oil was being used. From these three sources the results seemed to spring.

Shortly after the President was announced to be using the oil, Dr. Carver revealed that he had been treating two Georgia boys for paralysis. The lads regularly made the trip for their treatment. As the newspapers popularized the use of the oil as a cure, Dr. Carver said, "It has been given out that I have found a cure. I have not, but it looks helpful. I gave some to women and they used it and said they seem to gain in the use of their withered members. I have used it on two hundred and fifty people and it never failed so far as I can find out. For certain things it has definite value, but for others it remains to be proven."

On April 11, 1934, he gave all the credit to God for whatever value there might be in the use of his oil for infantile paralysis sufferers, and refused to accept any honor for himself. Speaking extensively during that year at colleges and universities, he did not alter the spiritual tone of his message.

"We get closer to God as we become more intimately acquainted with the things He created," he said in these addresses, which were heard at Yale, New York University, the University of Pittsburgh, Howard University and scores of smaller institutions throughout Mississippi, Louisiana, Georgia and other Southern states. "I love to think of nature as an unlimited broadcasting station, through which God speaks to us every hour, if we will only tune in. Pursue truth with a new zest and give all the credit for the answers to the greatest of all teachers."

The Washington *World* summarized his reception in all these places when it characterized his address at Howard University by saying, "The student body was electrified."

Tuskegee has been honored by famous visitors, including many of the famed persons living during the period of its history, as for instance, Theodore Roosevelt, who served upon its board of trustees for years, and President Franklin Delano Roosevelt, who visited Dr. Carver in his laboratory. But it is doubted whether any of these visitors were received more cordially than a famous man whom the doctor knew as a lad during his Ames apprenticeship.

In September, 1933, Vice-President Henry Wallace, then Secretary of the Department of Agriculture, took time out of his many duties to visit with his old professor and friend. This proved an enjoyable occasion for the two, when each in his own words and methods journeyed down memory's lane to the beginning of their friendship, when Carver, young and ebony-hued, was trailed through the greenhouses and the fields of Iowa by the small-fry Henry.

Speaking to the Methodist women of Columbus, Georgia, Carver used one of his famous subjects, "Through Nature to God," and as was often his method, the address was illustrated by the processes through which God's handiwork declares the glory of the Almighty. In many of these addresses he pointed out vividly the correlation of science and the Bible, introducing this fact, as he did in his 1939 annual chapel lecture on the subject, "Science and the Bible," by stating that both science and the Bible show the world to have been gaseous. With a lump of clay he indicated the fact that the second step was inert matter, void of plant life, to be followed by a stage wherein sea life was evidenced. Holding up before the audience a dinosaur tooth, found a thousand miles inland, he said, "There is no conflict between Genesis and geology or any true science."

A Carver story often told during these "depression" years points to the shrewdness of his humor. He always had an intense interest in cotton, even going so far as to form it into the foundation for roadmaking, but he in nowise was willing to accept King Cotton as a substitute for the cold cash he had been able to bank.

Up till 1912 or 1913, he could truthfully write to Booker T., "I have no bank account." But in his later years even the small salary of one thousand dollars annually was more than he could spend, and so he opened an account with a Tuskegee bank. When the crash of 1929 wrecked the banking structure of the nation, the local bank, holding all the doctor's life savings, went under. As the years progressed, the wise financiers were able to salvage some of the lost money. Much of this came in the form of cotton accepted in lieu of cash loan payments.

The directors held a meeting and decided to pay their depositors in cotton. They sent word to the various persons whose accounts they had not been able to make good, asking if they would accept cotton for the cash.

"Will you accept cotton for cash?" the bank representative asked Dr. Carver in the thirties. The doctor stood quietly for a moment, an ashen hue marking his serious face, and then in his high soprano voice said, "I did not put cotton in the bank, and I am not willing to take cotton out." That settled the matter. Carver wanted the money, and, with others, later a great share of his deposits were so paid.

The doctor had nooked away in a hidden pigeonhole of his mind a particular place where he wanted that cash to spend its active working years; he wished to devote it to the establishment of the George Washington Carver Foundation that the research which he had inspired might be carried on through the decades.

Many times the scientist was asked to speak over the radio. His first appearance on a coast-to-coast broadcast came on December 27, 1935, when he was a guest of the "Strange As It May Seem" program, carried by the Columbia Broadcasting Company. Two years later on August 20 he told his life story over the National Broadcasting Company's chain of stations, with Edgar Guest acting as master of ceremonies. The subject was, "It Can Be Done."

Again on November 2, 1939, he and Joe Louis appeared on the "We the People" broadcast, which was sponsored by the American Legion Convention from Chicago, with Colonel Theodore Roosevelt serving as the master of ceremonies. During the same year he also spoke on the "Strange As It May Seem" broadcast.

In each of these addresses he gave the highlights of his career and revealed to the radio public something of the magic of his work.

In 1935 it looked as if the government would lure him to Washington, D. C., for on September 25 it was announced that he was officially appointed by the United States Department of Agriculture as collaborator in the Bureau of Plant Industry, Division of Mycology and Disease Survey. When asked if he would leave for Washington, he shook his white-topped head and said, "No, I prefer to remain at Tuskegee." As he had refused other offers to move, this one could not budge him from the Institute post. It was possible, however, for him to perform the duties of his new appointment and remain at Tuskegee, which he did.

He was now nearing the seventy-five mark, working, as he expressed it, on "borrowed time." Daily he sought to renew his strength at the divine fountain of assistance, and each morning as he read the Bible, communed with his Creator, either in the woods or his simple suite at Rockefeller Hall, he relied upon the divine promise, "As thy days, so shall thy strength be . . . " His calls were far more than he could fulfill, and only a scant few of the invitations to speak throughout the nation did he accept.

He did find time to continue experiments as they rushed to his mind, and even announced that he had discovered thirty different kinds of cattle feed available in the South, saying, "I am going to work out a balanced ration for dairy cows, one especially for production of milk, another for production of cheese, and then another feed for beef cattle for producing meat."

And on September 5, 1935, hogs came in for their attention, when he handed the farmer a list of balanced hog-menus, but he failed to say whether one was for bacon production, another for enlarging hams, another for pig's feet, and the fourth for producing bigger strips of belly in the sows, so that the "Southern poor white trash" could have larger hunks of sow's belly to boil with their wild vegetables and roadside weeds, which he had taught them were edible.

Had he turned his attention to such insignificant details, doubtless he could have done it; for the Chicago Meat Packers asked him, on October 25, 1935, to make a study of their problems of raising beef in the South, an item which he tucked in between folds of his manifold duties. When the government decided to use his sweet potato starch as the mucilage on postage stamps it gave him a mental uplift, for here again one of his products proved that it was able to take whatever lickings the nation would give it.

God had opened the treasures of truth to this ebony scientist, whose trust was wholly in Him. What others declared impossible, Professor Carver, under divine guidance, was able to discover. For all these impossibles - made - possible he asked no glory nor sought even to be paid for his achievement. He was humble, for back in his Kansas days he had discovered the Pearl of Great Price in whose steps he followed diligently. The greater the nation's applause, the meeker he became, for he felt that to open nature's secrets by his genius he must be as a little child, whose hand was in the Heavenly Father's.

He took his religious life seriously, and this divine leadership, which he often mentioned as the source of his accomplishments, was a living reality to him. Dr. Robert Bell, closely associated with Dr. Carver during the last decade of the scientist's life, tells of numerous visits in which he and the professor often prayed together.

"He believed the Bible to be God's Word," said the minister, "and he looked to Jesus Christ as his personal Saviour, through whose death he had been made spiritually alive. When I visited him in his laboratory, he would often bow his head, sitting at the desk, and speak to God as to a person present in the room. When he prayed thus it was like being in the vestibule of heaven."

Dr. Carver's Favorite Passages . . .

"Ye shall know the truth, and the truth shall make you free"
— John 8:32.

"In all thy ways acknowledge him and he shall direct thy paths"— Prov. 3:6.

"Study to shew thyself approved unto God, a workman that needeth not to be ashamed, rightly dividing the word of truth"— II Tim. 2:15.

"I can do all things through Christ which strengtheneth me"
— Phil. 4:13.

"Where there is no vision, the people perish"— Prov. 29:18.

"Try these," said the doctor to his students, "and see what a marvelous vision will come to you."

Dr. Carver's Prayer . . .

"May God ever bless, keep, guide and continue to prosper you in your uplifting work for humanity, be it great or small, is my daily prayer. And may those whom He has redeemed learn to walk and talk with Him not only daily or hourly, but momently through the things He has created."

L.

Chapter VIII

SETTING HIS HOUSE IN ORDER

"If I hadn't discovered you," said Dr. Carver during the last summer of his life to his first and only assistant, Austin W. Curtis, Jr., "I wouldn't be living now."

The scene was the laboratory-office of the Carver Museum. Sitting back of the famous Carver desk, littered with papers and unfinished business the scientist left, was Dr. Curtis, upon whom the departed scientist's mantle had fallen only six weeks previous. I touched the Carver Bible, which had comforted the doctor through more than fifty years of struggle and had been with him during the decades of triumph and world acclaim.

"Leave it just where it is," said the man who now heads the Carver Museum and to whom the doctor left the task of finishing what he had only begun to do. I recalled his words, "I have only scratched the surface. It remains for those coming after me to dig deeper than I have ever been able." The young scientist's tone broke through my revery and, crystallizing his thoughts into words, I heard him say, "That is where Dr. Carver kept the Bible, and it shall always remain right there."

"In reality," I broke in, rudely forgetting conversational right-of-ways, "it was living for the purpose of indoctrinating you in his technique and training you to carry on his researches which extended his life during these past seven and a half years?"

The younger scientist sat for a moment with a seriousness holding his words in check and then said, "Yes. But it is a tremendous responsibility for me to carry. The strength that I have for the task is the fact that he believed I could do it. He knew how to get at the heart of problems, never worrying about nonessentials, and all of his work was strictly utilitarian, for some specific purpose. This also shall be our goal."

So manifold were the investigations, so numerous the products he fabricated from Macon County's and the South's ready-at-hand materials, that should Dr. Curtis achieve no more than formulate, bring to light and make available for current usage all of Carver's findings he will be a worthy successor to the man who discovered him.

There was no let-up in the Carver work during the last three-quarters of a decade. He was America's outstanding agricultural chemist, long since so honored and rightly recognized, and as such his presence on any lecture platform, at any exhibition or fair demanded a large audience both of curiosity seekers and interested spectators. But this did not give him the heart-push which tided him over the eighty mark. Carver had always been a lone scientific-wolf. He did not travel well with the pack, as his relationship to Bridgeforth shows. He planned and thought out his work in communion with nature and nature's Creator. In his laboratory no assistants ran tests, concocted minor brews, set vats bubbling with chemical stews. All of this the doctor insisted on doing for himself.

When he arrived at the stopping time around seventy-three, he realized that his work would suddenly come to an end at his death. He faced the important question: Shall I finish as I have worked all these years — alone? Or shall I find an assistant whose thinking and *modus operandi* I shall shape by my own hand that he may carry on where I leave off?

The decision made, Carver began the quest which ended one day when he saw the young scientist Curtis, and he said to Dr. Patterson, once removed from the president's chair occupied by Booker T. Washington, "That's the man I want." Here began a close relationship between teacher and understudy. From that time on, the old man and the younger were inseparable.

Scratch beneath the Carver surface and you would find Curtis, for now the doctor's dominant motive for living was that the Carver touch might be instilled into the young man's fingers. They traveled together, worked together in experiments, stood side by side in laboratories, and now Curtis began to perform for the doctor those tasks by which other assistants had always aided the scientists with whom they worked. Carver's prayer was that he might hold out, stretch the limited strength of his failing heart, until his assistant was trained in the Carver-way of working. When this was accomplished, like the last leaf on the tree, he faded away . . .

During the years many honors came to the scientist. The first to recognize his greatness was not his own nation but Great Britain. On November 29, 1916, the Royal Society for the Encouragement of Arts, Manufactures and Commerce, London, elected him a fellow of the old and honorable organization, which had been founded in 1754. Dr. Carver was justly proud of the certificate of membership which hung on his walls.

In 1923 he was awarded the Spingarn Medal, a gold medal which since 1914 has been annually awarded "for the highest and noblest achievement by an American Negro during the previous year." May 5, of the same year, the Daughters of the Confederacy gave honor to him, and he received a message stating that the members "send you a written expression of their interest and appreciation in your efforts to exhibit the products and possibilities of our South . . . and wish you Godspeed in any endeavor." As noted elsewhere, when the degree of Doctor of Science was awarded him in June of 1928, Professor Carver looked with joy upon the long-away term of study he had spent at the institution.

Doubtless he appreciated this his first honorary title, coming from his alma mater, more than the same degree which the University of Rochester awarded him on June 18, 1941, in the Tuskegee Chapel, at the hands of the Rochester president with the co-operation of Dr. Patterson.

His appointment as Collaborator, Mycology and Plant Disease Survey, Bureau of Plant Industry, Department of Agriculture, which came in September, 1935, was a gracious recognition of his services and leadership in this field. On October 28, 1939, the national committee awarded him the Theodore Roosevelt Medal for distinguished service to science. On one side of the medal is engraved the head of Theodore Roosevelt, and on the other a flaming sword, with the words, "If I must choose between righteousness and peace, I choose righteousness."

He traveled to New York City to receive the

medal, and John Hamilton, then chairman of the National Republican Committee, said in making the presentation, "You have brought great honor to all of us again and I beg to extend congratulations." He went to New York City simply clad, a flower in his buttonhole, and wearing a large necktie, "tied in a four-in-hand, not seen in New York City for a generation," said a local newspaper in reporting the incident.

Shortly before this he had been in New York City for an address, and had made reservations at the Hotel New Yorker, but when he arrived, the hotel refused to honor the reservations. For six hours the famous old ebony-hued scientist sat in the hotel. When the incident became known in the city, protests began to flow in, until the hotel was forced to relent its decision and give him the room. The publishers, Doubleday-Doran Company, telephoned and threatened to sue the hotel, and at the same time the New York *Post* contacted them and demanded action, which was soon coming. In this case, as always, the scientist was not forced to fight for himself.

On November 2, of the same year, he was selected by the *Herald Tribune* to speak at its Forum on National Problems, which was broadcasted over a national hook-up. While in the city, the doctor said, "One reason I never patent my products is that if I did it would take so much time I would get nothing else done. But mainly I don't want my discoveries to benefit specific favored persons."

If possible he attended awarding ceremonies when he was recipient of the honor. However, on May 10, 1940, the Fifth Convention of the International Federation of Architects, Engineers, Chemists and Technicians presented him with a plaque in recognition of his achievements, but the doctor was unable to attend the dinner. Sending his regrets, he commissioned his assistant Dr. Curtis to accept the award in his name.

"If this man, born in slavery, had not received the opportunity he rightly deserved, his contribution to the progress of the nation would have been lost," said the speaker in presenting the gift.

While there were many national honors that came to him, of which he could be rightly proud, doubtless none brought him more joy than one he received on February 17, 1941, from the Vernon, Texas, Presbyterian Church. There are several suggested reasons for his pride in accepting this award, but the explanation may be the little known fact that the doctor himself was a Presbyterian, which information is shared but by a few. He looked upon this membership in the League of the Golden Hearts, sponsored by the church previously mentioned, as a blessed award which greatly touched his heart.

"It is not often that I am given the happy assignment of writing such a letter as this one," said the church pastor, Dr. J. Albert Steele, in presenting the membership certificate. " . . . for never before in my eventful life has it been my happy lot to share in the conferment of a distinguished award upon one of the uncrowned Americans who has contributed much to the happiness and welfare of his fellow men.

"Over the years, unknown to you, your life has been observed closely by many persons who have rubbed elbows with you . . . As you have gone about the tasks of each day, even though the darkened hours of despair have now and then overcome you, you have not forgotten the Strength that has comforted you . . . This Strength has been manifest in efforts you have made in behalf of others in need . . .

"Your goodness has demonstrated the ardent character of your friendship . . . and your encouragement and faith . . . will keep ever burning before their faltering steps the kindly light of hope.

"Our earnest prayer is that the spirit of Him, in whose hands are the issues of life, may guide and richly bless you . . . until the last day."

In writing to Dr. Robert Bell, pastor of the Tuskegee Presbyterian Church (White), on March 6, 1941, Dr. Carver said, " . . . I appreciate your prayers and your interest which have meant so much in my upward struggle to regain my strength . . . " Enclosing the letter from the League of the Golden Hearts, he went on to say, "It is a beautiful and wonderful thing, just as wonderful as the letter, which is a masterpiece, and in so many ways sounds like the one that you wrote me."

It was Dr. Bell who accidentally discovered Carver's church relationship. One day the minister was speaking with a Senator and a local banker, when the scientist approached. Said the Senator, in asking Dr. Bell if he knew the Tuskegee sage, "He might be a Presbyterian."

"His scholarship, greatness, ability and the wonderful results of his life," returned the minister, in a complimentary tone, "make him eligible for Presbyterian membership." When the doctor was asked what church he belonged to, he said simply, "The Presbyterian."

This began a joyous relationship between minister and scientist which continued until Dr. Carver's death. During the scientist's many sicknesses, Dr. Bell was always a welcome visitor at his bedside. Many times when people went to the museum housing the doctor's laboratory, they were refused admission, but Dr. Carver left orders that whenever the minister came, he was to be brought immediately to him. Many were the intimate stories the minister carried away from those laboratory visits.

"One day I went to the laboratory to see Dr. Carver," related the minister to me while sitting in his study at Tuskegee, "and he told me how he discovered the long-lost Egyptian blue. 'I have found the blue which has been lost since the day of the Pharaohs,' he said. 'I have been working on it for a long time, but couldn't seem to get it right. Then I asked, Heavenly Father, what shall I do? He told me to add something to my mixture, and out came the lost Egyptian blue.' "

The spiritual note was dominant in these visits. Sitting at his desk, the scientist would bow his head and offer a prayer for the minister's health and the success of his work, asking the preacher to breathe a prayer for him as well. On one visit the doctor said, "People thought I wouldn't get well this last time I was sick. But I knew I would, for I had a life work to complete. But now it is done, and I am ready to go."

The Catholic Conference of the South, which met on April 22 of the same year, followed in the steps of the League of the Golden Hearts and awarded Dr. Carver their annual citation for service to humanity. The citation said:

"George Washington Carver . . . A great American who was born a slave, but has spent his every year freeing the minds of his countrymen of all that makes for interracial misunderstanding and un-Americanism. A genius in the laboratory, a father to his people, an inspiration to his fellow man, he has enriched the life of every American with uncounted inventions and good deeds, without enriching himself . . . All must be inspired by his example and leadership."

On the wall of Dr. Carver's laboratory, where several of these honors are seen, hangs a framed letter from President Franklin D. Roosevelt, dated April 7, 1939, in which he says, " . . . Yours has been a life of service of which the American people are proud . . . I do use the peanut oil from time to time and am sure it helps. Sincerely yours, Franklin D. Roosevelt."

As their contribution to the recognition and honors which were bestowed upon the scientist for his achievements, the Variety Clubs of America, in a meeting at Atlantic City, May 17, 1941, gave him the plaque for humanitarian services, which carried a stipend of one thousand dollars.

In all these tributes the scientist was rightly happy, though none of them seemed to alter the simplicity of his life and faith. He remained the unaffected man of achievement he had always been.

Many famous visitors came to see the peanut wizard at his laboratory during these latter years. In the spring of 1939 President Roosevelt took time out from his busy routine to meet the scientist at Tuskegee. He was on his way to Warm Springs, Georgia, and wanted to greet personally the man who had done so much to help infantile paralysis sufferers like himself. Vice-President Wallace shortly before had said, "Super ability is not the exclusive possession of any one race or any one class. When I was a small boy, George Carver . . . was a good friend of my father's . . . It was he who first introduced me to the mysteries of botany and plant fertilization."

A long friendship existed during the years between Ford and Dr. Carver, and on May 9, 1941, the industrialist and his wife stopped at the Institute, where, after showing the Fords through the Museum, James Lomax, the scientist's private dietician, served the company with a meal of wild vegetables, consisting of salads, sandwiches and other edibles, most of which came from the fields around the laboratory.

The last spring Dr. Carver was alive he returned the visit and spent some time with Dr. Curtis as Ford's guest at Dearborn, and it was rumored that at this time an attractive reward was promised for the scientist's services, if he would remain in the industrialist's employ. Dr. Carver denied any such intent, and when asked what they talked about, he replied, "We talked about many things. Mr. Ford is charming. It was such a pleasure to talk to him . . . But I belong to the South."

Deep in the scientist's heart lingered a desire to do something tangible to assure the continuity of his work. On June 2, 1937, the bust of Dr. Carver was unveiled as it stands before the entrance to his Museum, in honor of his forty years' work at Tuskegee. Dr. Thomas Turner of Hampton Institute was the special speaker for the occasion, and his address extoled the development of the Carver personality and ideal through the years as an example to other Negro youth. He was declared "the most outstanding Negro of all times," and newspapers, taking up the pean of praise, called him "the ebony Pasteur."

This set his mind wondering as to the investment which would provide the greatest possible humanitarian returns from his life savings, which by 1940 amounted to thirty-three thousand dollars. At the suggestion of Dr. Patterson he decided on February 13 of that year to endow the George Washington Carver Foundation with this money. In making the gift, he said, "I am sorry I am unable to give any more . . . " When one considers the meager salary he received, having refused gratuities for the services coming from all his discoveries and the tasks he did freely for whoever would call upon him for assistance, it is a testimony to his frugality that he had been able to save this amount.

He lived simply, spending cash only when absolutely necessary, and the Institute furnished him with board and housing during the many years of his association with its faculty. On June 30 he expressed the wish that his work would go on, and "I trust that the endowment fund for the Museum and its work will reach two million dollars." At the time he was ill, feeling that the end of his work was not far distant.

The following year on May 18, he gave the $1,000 stipend from the Variety Clubs' award along with another $662 dollars to the endowment fund. By September of the following year, 1942, when the ravages of the war were being felt, he thought it fitting that his final gift, consisting of $6,300 in war bonds, be added to the endowment fund, making the total of his own beneficence $40,000.

"I want the American people to know," he said, in

giving the war bonds to the fund, "that the Negro is just as interested in the outcome of the war as any other citizen."

Even though he sensed that the end was not far distant, the man who had brought secrets from clays, flowers, peanuts and sweet potatoes could not remain inactive when there was work to be done. He spoke during the last three or four years scores of times at various farm gatherings, universities and before the student body at Tuskegee. His message remained ever the same; as always, he extoled the virtue of depending upon God to lead one in the study of nature. When asked why he had rejected the magnificent offer Mr. Edison had made years earlier, his answer was characteristic of his entire life of service.

"God didn't charge for His work in making the peanut grow," he said in July of 1942, after the *Progressive Farmer* had named him Man of the Year, "and I can't charge for mine." When questioned why he refused to charge for his formulas, his response was the same through the years, "I believe if I would have charged for my work, or set a price on my formulas, I would have lost the gift."

His final labors were not only marked by speech making, but he could not forget his first love — scientific research. In 1939, he announced the production of a cheap paint made from the mixture of clay and motor oil, and he furnished free to all the technique by which anyone could make it. He said at the time, "The reason the Southern farmer does not paint his house is that he is too poor. I am furnishing him with a paint cheap enough to be in the reach of all." The year previous, with Dr. Curtis by his side, he made a linenlike fiber from weeds, with which he had been experimenting for twenty-five years. He started January of his seventy-eighth year by releasing to the press his method for making a very edible purée from the peanut, along with a note describing the weeds suitable for use as war substitutes for vegetables.

He escaped the lure of science long enough so that on November 24, 1941, his famous painting, *The Yucca*, could be unveiled in his Museum, where it now occupies a place of honor among the scores of paintings which are here displayed. This painting brought him the title of "the black Leonardo," as he had long ago been popularized as "the ebony Pasteur." During the first part of that year Henry Ford said of him, "He is the greatest living scientist. I have named our school here" — Ways, Georgia — "after him."

On February 15, Dr. Carver mentioned the intent of some of these compliments to Dr. Curtis, saying, "He is the first person I ever found who had the vision and inspiration to carry on my work." The doctor had named some of his pigments after his assistant, calling them "Curtis Browns." Working independently of Dr. Carver, though often under his direct supervision, Curtis during this time had made soaps, colors and perfumes from the magnolia tree, and, with Carver, had presented to the South a formula for cheap paint.

His interest in discovering uses for cotton continued strong, and on July 31, 1941, in an interview, he said he was testing cotton for road making, giving it an additional quality which would cause it to be weather-resistant. In an article on June 13 in the Montgomery *Advertiser* he told the farmers, who for many years had been reading his articles, that according to one of his recent investigations peanut hulls would solve their fertilizer problems.

During his last August, with Curtis' aid he turned over to the government, through the army, a successful camouflage paint which could be easily and cheaply produced. Nor could he forget gardens, wild vegetables and weeds to keep the nation's tables from feeling the pinch of war, and he gave to the public his "sour grass pie, which is not bad," as he described it.

When England had received his last bulletin, published in October, 1942, a member of Parliament said, "Parliament, when the war is won, should give thanks to Dr. Carver."

His mind was so geared to mental activity that it refused to stop. His body had withered to a slight, stooped form, his steps were slow, but as he continued to enter the laboratory, or daily to water his flowers, the giant that was in his mind kept active the creative processes which many years earlier had brought him fame, although he had refused the fortune attending it.

He had reached a time-honored old age. He had found another to whom he could entrust his work. It was as if he were ready to release his hands from his burden, for walking one day up the steps of the Museum to enter what to him for so many years had been "God's little workshop," he stumbled and fell . . . and the end was just beyond the bend of the hill.

From this time on he was confined to his room, and the worry which in his early Booker-T.-Washington days had often slipped to the surface of his mind, now was found to be needless; for tender hands were ever close by, ready to care for his needs. He had given his life for Tuskegee, and now when the end was in sight, Tuskegee friends were willing to do all in their power for him.

Constant in attendance was his boy Lomax, whom Uncle Sam had loaned the professor until the end, the hostess of Dorthy Hall, President Patterson and Dr. Curtis. The man who had enriched the world by his humble services was not to leave the world unblessed by the hands of friends.

He found consolation in the often-quoted Scripture passages he dearly loved, and, as Dr. Bell states, in his latter years he many times repeated Jesus' message of comfort, so applicable to him in these hours of need.

"Let not your heart be troubled: ye believe in God, believe also in me. In my Father's house are many mansions: if it were not so, I would have told you. I go to prepare a place for you . . ."

Dr. Carver was now ready to go to be with Jesus, through whose death he had been redeemed.

L.

Spiritually Strong . . .

" . . . He was spiritually strong. He believed that all science pointed to God. Through his profound spiritual life, his great scientific and artistic talents were awakened. He was a demonstration of the simplicity of eternal faith. He was a giant in the field of creative achievement."

-Spoken by Dr. Mary McLeod-Bethune, director of the National Youth Advancement for Negroes

"To enter this world a slave . . . and to become a practical chemist whose achievements were recognized by many honors — such was the career of George Washington Carver. A material age hailed him . . . Yet unlike these materialists . . . he was touched not only by something like genius but by a noble spirituality . . .

"He regarded himself an instrument in the hands of Providence . . . He might have died rich. Instead he gave his discoveries freely to the world . . . All Americans have reason to be proud of the dauntless spirit that triumphed over every handicap."

—Editorial in the New York *Times*

L.

Chapter IX

GOD'S SCIENTIST LAYS DOWN HIS BURDENS

"It is not we little men who do the work," said Dr. Carver a few years before his death, in expressing his religious philosophy upon which his achievements were based, "but it is our blessed Creator working through us . . . Other people can have this power, if they only believe. The secret lies" — touching his Bible which was on his desk — "right here, in the promises of God. They are real, but so few people believe them to be real."

This epitomizes the source of his power by which he obtained spiritual guidance for research. Often he quoted the Scripture, "I can do all things through Christ which strengtheneth me." Throughout his entire scientific career this spiritual note is dominant. It runs like a golden thread through his investigations and binds his results into a whole. Back of it all, he affirmed, stood God, upon whose directive power he relied for specific guidance in each investigation. Not that he did not throw upon every problem all his scientific acumen and ability, but using these native and acquired powers he asked God to lift them above the phase of human ordinariness and endow them with heaven-sent genius.

Early in the doctor's career, he learned the secret of success to be this search for true wisdom and divine guidance. From the beginning he was a careful student of the Bible, a practice which gave birth to his religious inclination. Early in his Tuskegee work several students, including his own office boy, entered his laboratory one day and asked him to teach them the Bible. From this came his famous Bible class which he conducted each Sunday for many years, relinquishing the task only when the burdens of age made it imperative. There were few Sundays before 1929 when he could not be found in the auditorium of what now is the Music Hall, surrounded by a hundred or so students to whom he unraveled the mysteries of God's Word.

"His teaching was specific and interesting," said one who for many years sat in the class. "He knew the Bible thoroughly, and made it a practice to illustrate his talks from the Word. He often acted out the part of the lesson under study. Many times he brought objects from the laboratory to make his instruction more impressive."

During Booker T. Washington's life, several ministers came to the president and complained about Carver's Bible class, saying, "He is more popular than we are, and he draws the people away from us." Booker T., a shrewd student of human psychology, asked, "Are they compelled to come?"

On being told that the students and friends went freely, the doctor inquired, "You say he has the auditorium full?" To which the preachers nodded assent, and Booker T. said, "Well, I guess I'll visit it myself," his eyes twinkling, "and if he is able to draw a crowd like that you boys had better take lessons from him."

Dr. Carver never thought of himself, in lecturing across the nation, as a preacher, but merely as a humble scientist who had been God-taught. However, in 1937, Glenn Clark invited him to Minneapolis to be one of the leading speakers at the city-wide Crusade for Christ, and as he delivered his "Mr. Creator, Why Did You Make the Peanut?" address, the audience sat spellbound, for the voice was that of one who had been long closeted with his Maker.

A familiar sight during the Institute's early history was that of Dr. Carver acting as one of the collection-takers at the Sunday services. He always insisted on attending these religious meetings as long as his strength permitted.

"When I visited him," relates Dr. Bell, who on many occasions stood by the scientist during the sicknesses of the last year of his life, "he always loved to talk about Jesus, the Parables, and would say 'A man's life consisteth not in the abundance of the things which he possesseth . . . but in doing the Father's will.' His humble greatness came from his willingness to be the servant of all, like Jesus said."

When people visited him at the laboratory, he would often sit at his desk and preach sermons to them. On one occasion Dr. Bell and Dr. Donald MacGuire, a Montgomery, Alabama, minister, went to see the scientist, and before they left his usual sermon was delivered with such effectiveness that both of the preachers felt they had been in a gospel meeting.

"I valued his prayers so much," a Southern minister affirms, "for God was real to him. He lived in the atmosphere of the divine presence. While quoting the passage with the words, 'reserved for you in heaven,' the doctor's eyes would fill, for he sensed the reality of what God was preparing for him."

He was so deeply religious that when he talked with those possessing a spiritual inclination they too felt God was near him. He had atmosphered his thinking in this realm so long that when he came to the end of his days, his last words were of a religious nature.

Until Christmas, 1942, he was able to be about; each day he visited his laboratory, and maintained a vital interest in the people whom he contacted. Many were the students who told me of some encouraging word he spoke to them as he was going to and from "God's little workshop."

James Lomax, "his boy," as Dr. Carver affectionately termed him, carefully tended to the doctor's meals, and when during the last ten days he was confined to the room, and to a large chair, for he could not lie down, James was not for long out of calling distance. And near by also was the hostess of Dorthy Hall. James had been with Carver four years, and for months the doctor had carefully "graded" each meal prepared by the young dietician. When he had completed what the doctor thought was his "course," he gave the young man a Certificate of Merit, printed in his own hand and decorated with Carver paintings.

On Christmas Eve, the scientist, confined to his room, said to James, "Lomax, don't forget you are to play Santa Claus for me." Therefore on the following day James delivered the cards which Dr. Carver had made, and also the presents, and for James there was a handmade tie as a gift in recognition of his kind services. So close was this relationship between scientist and young dietician that when James was drafted, Dr. Carver said, "I don't see how I can live without you," and the army, hearing the appeal of the aged scientist, deferred the lad until after the doctor should need him no longer.

On the last day of his life, about four in the afternoon, Dr. Carver asked, "What are you doing?" to be answered by James, "Preparing your meal."

"Yes, they are also preparing for me in the other world," came the final words to be uttered by George Washington Carver.

By seven-thirty that evening, January 5, 1943, the frail little man, sitting in the large comfortable chair which kind hands at Tuskegee had furnished, breathed his last, and he entered the other world about which he had spoken so much, and met face to face the Creator with whom he had talked and by whom he had been guided in making the marvelous discoveries which marked his long and honored career.

His body lay in state from ten o'clock Thursday until two-thirty the following afternoon when the funeral was conducted in the Tuskegee chapel, in which he had sat so many times during his career at the Institute. Telegrams arrived from famous people throughout the nation, as well as from those lesser known persons whose careers had been shaped by the scientist's now-stilled hands.

When the hour arrived for the service, there was no standing room in the chapel. By the altar stood his casket, mounded by flowers. The floral piece which covered his casket had been furnished by Mrs. Henry Ford, and a personal representative of the industrialist was in attendance at the service.

In the lapel of his coat was a beautiful camellia, the gift of a white lady whom years before the doctor had befriended. Dr. Claude M. Haygood of Tuskegee told me the story of that camellia, a story which but few know.

"Years earlier," said the minister, "Dr. Carver was

asked by a lady to look at a dead camellia bush in her yard. On going in, the scientist studied the bush for some time and then went to his laboratory, where he prepared the proper medicine for it. Taking it to the lady, he treated the bush as a doctor would a sick child. And the following year blooms appeared again on it.

"Every year from that time on, when the first bloom burst, the lady would take it to Dr. Carver as a present. And when he died, the friend requested the privilege of furnishing a camellia from the bush he blessed into life again. There in his buttonhole, where he always wore a flower when alive, it was but fitting that a camellia should grace his body in death."

Dr. Haygood read the beautiful words of the Beatitudes. President Patterson delivered a short *In Memoriam* address, expressing the common sentiment of all present: "God's greatest scientist, by arising from slavery to world fame, is an example to youth everywhere." Chaplain Richardson took as his theme the Golden Text of the Bible, "For God so loved the world . . . "

Softly the Institute choir lifted the words which to the doctor had been so inspiring in life: "On a hill far away stood an old rugged cross . . . So I'll cherish the old rugged cross, till my trophies at last I lay down . . . "

Kind hands carried his body out to burial in the little cemetery just behind the Chapel, where soon soft grasses and beautiful flowers shall spring up as an emblem of the fact that for God's great scientist, *death was a leap into the light*!

James Lomax, his "boy," expressed a sentiment to me which crystallizes the thought of the world — "I miss him so much."

L.M.J
April 13, 1957

PRINTED IN THE UNITED STATES OF AMERICA.